Thank God for a Funny Face

Published by John Blake Publishing Ltd,
3 Bramber Court, 2 Bramber Road, London W14 9PB, England

First published in hardback in Great Britain in 2002

ISBN 1 903402 50 6

British Library Cataloguing-in-Publication Data:
A catalogue record for this book is available from the British Library.

Typeset by Jon Davies

Printed in Great Britain by CPD, Wales

1 3 5 7 9 10 8 6 4 2

Papers used by John Blake Publishing Ltd are natural, recyclable products made from wood grown in sustainable forests. The manufacturing processes conform to the environmental regulations of the country of origin.
Pictures reproduced by kind permission of The Chester Chronicle, Zoe Dominic, MSI, The Richmond and TwickenhamTimes, Radio Times.

Thank God for a Funny Face

Hugh Lloyd

JOHN BLAKE

To my darling Shân,
without whom this book would never have been.

Contents

Foreword

I have always been a Hugh Lloyd fan. I watched him on television with Tony Hancock and heard him many times on the radio. In the mid-Eighties, while both of us were working at the National Theatre, I got a chance to meet him one day in the theatre canteen. I was so thrilled just to be able to say hello and introduce myself and he was so pleasant and I particularly got a kick out of it when he said, 'Nice to meet you, Tony.' (I've always been a fan of actors and especially greatly gifted 'comedians'.)

In my humble opinion, the great comic geniuses like Tony Hancock, Sid Field, Tommy Cooper, Morecambe and Wise, Charlie Chaplin, Laurel and Hardy, Ken Dodd,

Les Dawson, Jacques Tati and many others are far superior to the 'great, important classical actors' of our time — and I think Hugh Lloyd belongs there in the ranks of these great comedic artists.

In 1994, I was preparing to direct a film based on Chekhov's *Uncle Vanya*. The screenplay had been adapted by Julian Mitchell, and was set in North Wales at the end of the nineteenth century. There is one character in the screenplay called Pocky and, as Julian Mitchell and I were preparing the script, Hugh Lloyd's face kept popping up in my mind; so, not wanting to be too pushy, I wrote him a letter and asked if he would consider reading the script. I received an immediate response saying, 'Yes, please.' I was thrilled.

The summer of 1994 was so pleasant and the filming went well. As a director, I wasn't quite sure whether to direct the actors or just leave them alone to get on with it! Well, I took one look at Hugh during the rehearsal and thought, There is nothing to do here, just let him get on with it — he knows exactly what to do, so I'll just keep my big mouth shut. And Hugh Lloyd did just that — he got on with it! And what a superb performance it was — touching, hilariously funny and deeply sad and lonely.

I know very little of anything, but watching an actor like Hugh Lloyd perform, something inevitably comes through — a deep, fundamental grasp of the ridiculousness of the human condition, with its priceless self-importance, its futile struggle in an incomprehensible world. I suppose that's what acting is all about; and Hugh Lloyd is an exquisite example of this gift, this talent to amuse — to break one's heart.

Sir Anthony Hopkins

Ladies and Gentlemen ...

Comedy — it's a funny business. What I mean is, apart from, say, music or football, it's the only job I can think of where the people you admire — your heroes — you may get to meet them and, if you are really lucky, even work with them.

I had the opportunity recently of working with one of my heroes of comedy — the great Hugh Lloyd.

Throughout the rehearsals for my BBC show, the scriptwriters and I were writing and rewriting, as is the usual practice in the process of a sitcom, to see what worked and vice versa. The biggest compliment for me was not only his agreement to do our script, but his enthusiasm and willingness to contribute to the show. Hugh would be given new versions of his scenes on a daily basis and he would disappear into a corner and return with notes all over the page with much funnier lines.

After a few days, when I felt that Hugh was more relaxed, I seized my chance and plied Hugh with a million questions about his life.

I couldn't help myself because the stories he told about the people he had worked with and the things that had happened to him were so interesting. I loved listening to his stories about the Old Windmill Theatre in London and the time he spent working with the great Tony Hancock; the digs he stayed in; the shows he had done — it was fascinating.

Throughout rehearsals and until the Friday night when the show was recorded, I had the privilege of watching him work and then there I was with Hugh on the TV set.

This may sound mushy, but I really enjoyed watching Hugh work — his sense of timing, his delivery, his professionalism in interpreting our lines — he neither did too much nor too little.

Thank you, Hugh, for the great week you spent with us. You are a fantastic bloke and a brilliant comedian — you made us laugh a lot.

Good luck, my friend.

Lee Evans

I knew Hugh was a fine comic actor but was not prepared for the definitive Chekhovian performance he gave as Firs in *The Cherry Orchard* at the National. He moved me to tears every night. He is like a rock on stage — nothing throws him. He's an invaluable actor to have in a company — supportive and generous. As he is in life. A dear loyal friend. I love him.

Sheila Hancock

I shall always treasure the memories of working with Hugh at the Royal National Theatre in Chekhov. It was good to make Hugh legitimate at last!

Sir Ian McKellen

Question: What does Hugh Lloyd have in common with a Welsh bee-keeper, a down-at-heel man of the people, a lion and an impoverished member of the aristocracy with a penchant for appearing in drag?

Answer: *Everything*. He makes every character real. A performer with no ego but what an enormous amount of talent.

John Nathan-Turner
(TV and Theatre Producer)

Prologue

At the height of his stardom, Hugh volunteered to return to his native Chester to help boost a new theatre project there by appearing unpaid in a poignant play called *Rattle of a Simple Man*.

The plot centred around a Northern football fan, a virgin in his 40s, who is dared by his pals on a visit to London to pay for the services of a prostitute.

The theatre was directly opposite the Welsh chapel where he was brought up, and the ladies of the chapel decided that instead of their yearly outing to a Liverpool theatre they would go along and support their local star.

Hugh's mum thought she had better warn them that the

action took place in a prostitute's flat.

On hearing this, there was a momentary pause ... and then, with a beam, the minister's wife said brightly, 'Well, if it's Hugh, it'll be all right, won't it?'

1

Kings and Queens – My Chester Childhood

I suppose it had to happen that the news of my arrival into the world was made on a theatre stage! Although I wasn't born into a professional theatrical family, my mother was an excellent pianist and music teacher who was well-known and loved in the amateur operatic circles of my home town of Chester.

On 23 April 1923, the day after I was born, the Chester Operatic Society were staging the musical comedy *The Arcadians*, set in a very happy place called Arcadia. But there was one miserable character in the show, a jockey called Simon Doody, who on this particular occasion was being played by the local optician, Alf Siddall. He made an extraordinary entrance, on a real horse, which, of course, could be pretty dangerous at times, in more ways than one.

He used to sing a song in a very mournful voice, with a doleful face. It went, 'I've gotta motta ... always merry and bright.'

When he'd finished his song at this particular performance, he leant down from the horse and whispered to the assembled company, 'Maggie Jones has had a boy!'

Yes, that was me! Hugh Lewis Lloyd.

Of course, Maggie Jones was now Maggie Lloyd, having married my father exactly nine months previously at the Queen Street Wesleyan Chapel in Chester. So it appears I was a honeymoon baby! As it turned out, I was to be an only child but I can't remember ever having felt lonely or wishing I had a brother or sister. I had friends, of course, but I was quite content being left to my own devices.

Home was a double-fronted terraced house — number 7, Raymond Street, a stone's throw from the centre of the Roman walled city. The house was called *Bryn Isa*, meaning 'small hill', which was appropriate as we looked straight across the canal to Moel Famau, the mountain which could always be identified as it had a sort of pimple mound on the top of it and, in the distance, the Welsh hills. In the Thirties, the view was spoilt by the erection of more houses opposite.

At a time when middle-class snobbishness was at its height, my mother delighted in the fact that Raymond Street had terraced houses and that we were the first that was double-sided. I can vividly remember our home always being full of music, song and laughter with a constant procession of my mother's piano pupils to and from the door. When my dad retired, I remember him saying he ought to get himself a uniform as my mother was forever sending him to open the front door!

Dad, Robert Lewis Lloyd, was a commercial traveller for a Chester tobacco manufacturer. He used to travel around North Wales in a horse-and-trap selling tobacco products — Bacco'r Bugail (Shepherd's Tobacco), Earl of Chester hand-made cigarettes and the ordinary ones called Auld Lang Syne. In later life, he was made manager of the factory that stood on the banks of the River Dee and, every day, regardless of the weather, would walk the one-and-a-quarter miles to work, then come home for lunch, then back again and then walk home at the end of the day. I was caught smoking cigarettes when I was about nine but he didn't make a fuss. He calmly gave me a cigar, hoping I would be sick and be put off smoking for life. It didn't work! I didn't suffer any unpleasant side-effects and progressed from pinching his cigarettes to pinching his cigars instead. Unfortunately, I've been a smoker, on and off, ever since, but when I meet anti-smokers who start criticising, I point out that I wouldn't be here today if it wasn't for tobacco as both my father, and my paternal grandfather, Lewis Lloyd, worked in the business. Well, that's my excuse!

In fact, the only advice I ever had from my father was not ro relight cigarette stubs and never ever to play cards with strangers!

The first time I got drunk was another matter entirely. I was 16 and had been to a party with some friends and over-indulged. As public transport wasn't widely available, everybody walked everywhere. I managed to stagger home, contemplating how narrow our road was, and tried to pull myself together as I reached the front door. My dad opened it and, attempting to look sober, I managed to totter past him, mumbling 'Goodnight', and realised I had to get to the bathroom ... quickly! I would have got away with it but for the fact that once inside the bathroom I promptly fell straight into the bath, bringing the entire contents of the bathroom cabinet down on top of me. That is how my dad found me and, as he could never bring himself to tell people off, he just didn't speak to me for the next two weeks, which was far worse.

Another juvenile drinking escapade happened on a school trip to Paris. It's the only time in my life I have lost an entire day. It was the first time I had ever tried Pernod — I had three. I couldn't remember a thing. But on that trip I did get to go and see that wonderful entertainer Maurice Chevalier, and he received the longest ovation I have ever witnessed.

Living with us at Raymond Street was my maternal grandmother, Nainy. She was a tiny old lady with striking looks and an equally striking personality, with strong religious beliefs and high moral principles. My mother and father, out of respect for her, I suppose, never had any drink or Sunday newspapers in the house! In this day and age, it might seem strange that the grandmother should dominate her daughter and son-in-law in this way, but anyone who has had a chapel upbringing, like myself, will realise that it is an exclusive club with its own set of rules. I adored Nainy but, as I grew older, I used to argue with her on all sorts of issues. I used to say that if you shouldn't have newspapers on a Sunday then you shouldn't have them on a Monday either — which we did — because people had worked on Sunday to produce them. But she wasn't having any of it.

Of course, anything that was banned became a curiosity for a young boy like myself and fortunately help was at hand next-door through our neighbours, Aunty Margaret, Aunty Lil and Uncle Harry, who used to let me read their Sunday papers — *Reynolds News*, *Empire News*, the *News of the World* and the *Sunday Pictorial* — safely away from Nainy's eagle eye! Sunday was a regular routine — boiled eggs for breakfast, a mile-long walk to chapel and back and then Sunday dinner in the dining-room.

In the afternoon, we would sleep or read then walk to chapel and back in the evening, arriving home for Sunday supper which consisted of the cold left-overs from our dinner! We would listen to the wireless — but only religious programmes — read a verse from the Bible and then I would go to bed, just glad that the weekdays were about to start. I suppose I had a strict upbringing, though I can honestly say I never felt I had anything but a happy home life.

Nainy lived with us until she died in her nineties but even now her 'doings and sayings' live on in our home. For instance, if I feel guilty about sitting down doing nothing I always remember what Nainy used to do. She would rise firmly to her feet and say, 'This and worse will never do but this and better may.' And off she would go to make herself busy.

I started school at the Queen's School kindergarten,

where the girls far outnumbered the boys, especially in playground fights! One of my earliest memories is of one of my more formidable classmates, a girl called Marjorie, who unfortunately — and I'm not sure why — had only one arm. However, Marjorie was not in the least bit deterred by this seeming disability; in fact, she looked on it as a definite advantage in the school playground. I have never since come across a more fierce fighting weapon than the stump of her arm! She would lash about in all directions, forcing her opponents to scatter in terror.

It was at the Queen's School that I was first struck by Cupid's arrow! The object of my boyhood passion was my lovely, blue-eyed teacher Miss Draper. Alas, she never knew of my love and it remained unrequited!

In the late Twenties, when I was about six or seven, we sometimes used to go on the bus for a day out to the seaside, the North Wales resort of Rhyl. We would take the Crosville bus, which stopped at the bottom of the road, to Rhyl bus station. To me, that bus station became a gateway to paradise, knowing that the seashore was just a short walk away from the town. Full of excitement, I would head for the sands to see Jackie the donkey boy and his donkeys and have a ride, then play in the sand and throw pebbles in the sea until, reluctantly, I would return to the bus station.

One Sunday, on the promenade, dressed up like Little Lord Fauntleroy as I had come straight from chapel, I threw a handful of sand at a well-dressed lady who was strutting along on her Sunday constitutional. I don't know why I did it but she was furious. I, however, was quite delighted with myself and happily content with my well-deserved slap!

But the real highlight of the year was our annual summer holiday in the tiny North Wales seaside resort of Llanfairfechan — a place which was to play a major part in my destiny. Llanfairfechan. You would be hard pressed to find a more unlikely place to light the fires of burning theatrical ambition than this nondescript town tucked away between the bustling coastal playgrounds of Llandudno and Bangor. But it was here when I was about seven years old that I remember looking out across the sea and vowing to myself, 'One day, I will be an entertainer.'

It was with Mum and Nainy that I went for those long, lazy summer weeks. Dad worked long and hard all year so that his family could enjoy the break, and he would try and join us at the weekends — and before leaving for Chester, he would take me and the other children I was friendly with to choose our sweets for the week!

We used to take rooms in a big house called Menai Bank, a stone's throw from the sea. Alongside the lane outside the house ran a picturesque babbling brook and one of my greatest joys was that I could hear it from the window of my room as I lay in bed.

At first, I was just like the other children my age, happy playing with my toy boat or paddling in the sea ... but then I discovered a whole new world of my own.

On the promenade at Llanfairfechan there was a little seaside pavilion and I discovered there was a concert party who rehearsed and performed their shows there. They were men and women worlds away from anything my young eyes had ever encountered before. Perhaps it was the smell of the grease-paint, the sight of the costumes or maybe they just seemed to speak in a different way from anyone else I had ever known. Whatever it was, I was hooked.

I would stand and watch them coming and going and would beg my mum to let me go and see every show. To this day, the theatre building still stands proudly on the seafront, although it is now a café and souvenir shop, but it still means more to me than any West End theatre ever could.

I can also remember an occasion when I was ten years old, I was standing at a bus stop in Northgate Street in Chester with my 'Aunty' Florrie, a neighbour and close friend of my mum's. The stop was outside a church which had a Wayside Pulpit with a quotation and a date after it. It said 55BC. I said to Aunty Florrie, 'I'm going to be one of those.'

'One of what?' she replied, mystified.

'A "BC",' I said.

'And what's a BC?' she asked.

'Best Comedian,' I replied, with all the confidence of my ten years. And I'm still trying!

Back home, my world started to revolve around the theatre. When I was eight, I actually put on a ten-minute pantomime with 40 scenes which I wrote, directed and starred in! I also condescended to hand out a few parts to my friends. It was at this time that I managed to win a scholarship to the King's School, which was then housed in part of Chester Cathedral.

The actual building was originally a monastery which

was shut down and converted into a school by Henry VIII in 1541. The school has since been rebuilt on the outskirts of the city.

My eight years as a pupil there didn't leave me with any dazzling academic achievements, but I did win a great personal victory by overcoming a bad stammer to win the Orations Prize in my first year and my last year at the school. It's an affliction I've battled and coped with throughout my acting career.

I was never much good at sport, either — although I've always adored watching football, but that's another chapter. I did discover, though, that there is great merit in coming last. You find that the winner of a race always gets a big cheer, but the poor old loser, puffing in at the end, gets an even bigger ovation from the crowd! I got my school certificate but I have to confess that the only way I passed some of the subjects was because of the photographic memory I have. I only had to look at the page of a book and I could remember it. Of course, it's been a wonderful advantage to me while learning scripts.

Looking back on some of my old school reports, I discovered such phrases as 'must concentrate more' and 'needs more sleep' cropping up over and over again. This was because the theatre still remained the focal point of my life. As I got older, I started organising my own concert parties and learned at a very early age the advantage of knowing the right people! My mother had founded a very respectable choral group — the Deva Ladies Singers — and I eventually persuaded her to let me do my act at one of their performances at the very posh Grosvenor Hotel in the city centre. She agreed to let me go on ... in the interval when everybody was drinking their cups of tea and talking! You could see how much faith she had in me!

When it was time to leave school, I was hell bent on going into showbusiness but, although I met with no opposition from my parents, Dad wanted me to learn a 'proper' job to fall back on. The options were banking or journalism ... so I opted to join the world of newspapers.

2

Lloyd of the Chronicle

The *Chester Chronicle* shop, selling papers, classified advertising and prints of photos that had appeared in the paper, was on Bridge Street right in the heart of the city centre. But to get to the editorial offices, we reporters had to climb the steps up to the Rows — the covered, tiered walkways of shops that the city is so famous for — and make our way down a little passage wedged between The Etonian (a shop selling men's and boys' clothes) and the umbrella shop, into a little lane where the entrance to my new career was through the first door on the right. A little further along was the access to the printing works.

We cub reporters — I was 16 when I joined the staff — were housed in a tiny, freezing cold room with only a one-bar electric fire to keep us warm.

It was here that we were supposed to brush up on our shorthand when we weren't out on such exciting assignments as covering funerals, council meetings or garden parties. The unreadable handwriting I have today is probably derived from those early days on the *Chronicle* as my shorthand ended up as a cross between longhand and scribble! The floor above us housed the main newsroom where the senior reporters and the sub-editors were situated and where the Chief Reporter, George Roberts, reigned over 'The Book' — the diary of our assignments for the day.

Up another flight of stairs was the Editor's domain — the Holy Sanctum. This was presided over by the somewhat eccentric, old-school editor Frederick Parker. He was almost a caricature of himself. He was never seen without his 'Anthony Eden' black homburg perched on his head and always wore a brown tweed suit. The advantage of him being two floors up was that the wooden stairs were very creaky and we could hear him coming down well in advance. This was a signal to put all cigarettes out as he absolutely loathed smoking.

For a man devoted to communications, Frederick Parker certainly had some curious tendencies; he found it hard to adjust to the innovation of the telephone.

He would sit in his office, the floor littered with page proofs, and if the phone rang and there was a lady on the other end he would doff his hat to the receiver and say, 'Good morning.' One such lady who telephoned regularly and haunted the office was a local novelist called Beatrice Tunstall.

I think he eventually gave in and gave her a *Country Ways* column, but I well remember him doffing his Homburg at the telephone and saying, 'Good morning, Miss Tunstall.'

Frederick Parker lived in Bouverie Street, very close to my home in Raymond Street. This was a distinct advantage for me as we were supposed to be at the office around 9.00am, but we often weren't. I would watch from my bedroom window and wait to see him leave, then leap on to my bicycle and try to beat him to the office.

Over the three years I was at the *Chronicle* — from 1939 to 1942 — I tended to get more responsible jobs than a cub reporter such as myself would normally merit as most of the seniors were gradually called up for National Service. I was too young, of course, but I was desperate to do my bit and had my heart set on joining the RAF at the time. However, duty called at the paper, and I can remember on one occasion being sent to cover the funeral of a very important local big-wig. Of course, it was highly important to get the names of all the mourners as everybody wanted to see their name in the paper to show they had been there.

Also covering this prestigious ceremony was a friendly rival reporter from the opposition paper, the *Observer.* He was an old hack called Alex Holdey who more than enjoyed a tipple, and I was amazed that he could always provide a perfect account of any meeting in spite of seeming to be half-cut.

Holdey and I waited in the church porch to take the names of the people as they arrived for the funeral, and he appeared to have had more than a generous swig that day! As one mourner approached the door, Holdey stepped forward and asked his name.

'Jones,' replied the man.

Holdey dropped his notebook, picked it up with some difficulty then drew himself up to his full height and, breathing highly potent fumes over the startled man, barked, 'Do you think you are the only bloody Jones in Chester?'

My days as a reporter for the *Chronicle* were not generally filled with glamour and excitement, but I did manage to secure one celebrity interview — with the astrologer Gipsy Petulengro, who was visiting the city that week. At the time, I had passed my first RAF medical and was awaiting my second at RAF Padgate and was confident of getting into the services. After the interview, Gipsy Petulengro said to me, 'Would you like me to make a prediction for you?'

'Oh, all right,' I replied, pretending to sound like a nonchalant, worldly journalist who was not impressed.

'You will never fight in this war,' he said.

What absolute nonsense, I thought at the time as I was well on my way, it seemed then, to joining up. But as it turned out, he was right. Was it just a lucky guess, or was it something else? Of course, that's something I will never know.

My favourite job, of course, was covering Chester City, the local football team of which I have remained a life-long fan. Writing reports of their home fixtures taught me a lot about the Press, and I will look at my time as a Sports Correspondent and a Chester City fan in more detail in a later chapter.

Lloyd of the Chronicle

Although I was thoroughly enjoying my time in journalism, my heart still belonged to the world of entertainment. By now, I had founded the Chester Repertorygoer's Club and the Hugh Lloyd Repertory Revue Company. Of course, working on the *Chronicle* gave me the distinct advantage of being able to cover my own shows ... I have never had such glowing reviews and I frequently ran out of superlatives. Modesty was obviously not my forte at the time, for not long ago I came across an old theatrical notebook in which I describe myself as 'author, lyricist, composer, juvenile lead, entertainer, light comedian, compère, producer and publicity and press man', which rather leaves me wondering what on earth the rest of the cast were doing.

However, when I turned 18 I became eligible for the Forces and was ready and eager for action. I applied to join the RAF as I had intended and passed all the tests with flying colours ... until it got to the medical. Everything was fine, except for the fact that I had always suffered from chronic hay fever, and sneezed over every doctor I saw! So, sadly, they turned me down on account of the fact that they did not wish to entrust one of their bombers to somebody who was prone to a sneezing fit every two seconds.

My hay fever, which still remains with me today, has undergone every test and possible treatment in the book, including having all my teeth out at the age of 17 on the advice of the family doctor, whose word in those days was law. Needless to say, it did nothing at all except render me toothless!

Undaunted by my failure to become a pilot, I decided I could have a crack at being a spy. I wrote off to MI5 and quite astonishingly they wrote back, asking me up to Whitehall for an interview! So off I went up to London, accompanied by my dad. On the way there, we stopped to ask directions from a policeman, who turned out to be none other than film star Jack Hulbert who was a Special Constable.

The interview went well and they seemed very impressed by my enthusiasm but suggested tactfully that perhaps I was a little young and to come back in a year or two. I wasn't too bothered. I was still working on the *Chronicle* and, by now, other newspapers were covering my shows and concert parties.

I appeared in a Bright Black-Out Concert Party which won rave reviews and the coverage of my opening concert of the *War Follies of 1940* complimented me on my 'original ditties sung at the piano' and my 'witty impersonations' of 'Mr Winston Churchill, Vic Oliver, the Western brothers and an Irish comedian'. At the same time, I had formed a double-act with my old King's School chum Harvey Kirkpatrick. We called ourselves Doyle Devan and Scott Harvey and it was under these names that we made our very first professional appearance.

We were quite an intrepid duo and, finding an advert in *The Stage* which wanted acts to appear in Harry Cody's Circus at the Playhouse Theatre, Swindon, decided to apply.

It was to be my first proper audition but when it came to filling in the application form we were baffled by one of the questions. It said, 'Can you open and close in one?' Anyone familiar with theatrical terms will know this means 'Are you able to perform your act between the main curtains and a frontcloth, leaving the main stage area clear for the next act to set up?' This was to be my first lesson in the mystical language of showbusiness.

We hadn't a clue what it meant but, not wanting to appear inexperienced, put down 'Yes'.

It was only when our act was accepted that we started to worry about the possible outcome of this. So Harvey, using a phoney voice, rang up Jack Persich, the local theatre manager in Chester, to ask him what it meant. But our next lesson in 'showbiz speak' could have had far more drastic results. Wanting to appear worldly, we carried on confidently pretending we were old hands at the game. However, one of the female performers in the show was a woman of rather masculine appearance with very short-cropped hair. One night, she strode purposefully into our dressing room and asked, 'Are you two camp?' Not knowing what on earth she meant, we just replied, 'Oh, yes.' It wasn't until word spread around the company that we discovered the true meaning. It might seem naïve today but we genuinely hadn't a clue.

It was in shows like this where the meaning of the phrase 'the show must go on' became all too apparent. In the company were a mother and daughter team who did a bicycle act. For two nights, the girl went on with a badly sprained ankle, did the show and fainted in the wings when the act was over. But, of course, in those days there was also the saying 'no play, no pay', so it was little wonder some artistes went on until they literally dropped.

Leaving the cosy confines of Chester concert parties and going out into the real rat-race world of professional entertainment taught me the very great difference between professionals and amateurs.

When I was in my early teens, my mother used to try and make me put on an act for visitors in the drawing room and I used to freeze. I knew instinctively when it was the right time to perform and when it wasn't.

Amateurs, for instance, will gaily entertain anyone on stage or in the living room with friends. Professionals, I believe, are only happy when they are doing it in a professional atmosphere.

That is the difference between an amateur and a pro. Amateurs think they can be funny any way, any time. A pro knows when the time is right.

Although I had at last reached the dizzy heights of professional entertainment, I still wanted to do my bit for the war and ended up on a course as a Radio Operator for the Merchant Navy at the Wireless College in Colwyn Bay.

We had lots of free time as there was a shortage of ships so we used to go into nearby Llandudno in the hope of meeting some female company.

One of our greatest chat-up strategies (or so we thought) was pretending to be Norwegian sailors. The girls just flocked around us and it worked a treat until one night we were in a pub with two girls and some real Norwegian sailors walked in.

Most of my time at the Wireless College was spent

organising shows and concerts so it wasn't long before someone had the bright idea that, as I had spent most of my time entertaining my colleagues, I might as well go and entertain the troops.

And so I joined ENSA, known by the troops as Every Night Something Awful! My first audition for this admirable organisation was a little nerve-wracking as I had told them I could play the piano. In fact, my repertoire was limited to one tune — 'Red Sails in the Sunset'. Amazingly, I passed the audition and went into a show that only lasted two nights, which was a great relief to me as I might have been called on to play something else! From there, I joined George Thomas's Globetrotters, a troupe run by a husband-and-wife team, Teddy Harley and Patsy Crowther. I was to stay with them for the next three-and-a-half years until the end of the war, touring the whole of the British Isles, the Faroe Islands and Iceland.

I may not have fulfilled my dream of becoming an RAF pilot, but I felt sure I was doing more for the war effort than if I'd been taken on as a spy!

3

Flying Boats and Nazi Spies

Entertaining the troops. It was an exciting challenge and I was very much looking forward to travelling overseas again. And one of my first performances with the Globetrotters was certainly a memorable one. I was in the middle stages of having all my teeth out and had just undergone a removal session. The dentist, in order to bridge a temporary gap, had put dental putty in between two of my teeth, with the result that when I went on stage and said my first lines I promptly blew the putty straight into the commanding officer's face! My embarrassment over that little episode was soon superseded by the excitement of flying to the Faroe Islands in a Sunderland Flying Boat.

To my astonishment, the first sight that met my eyes

when we landed was a sign saying 'Chester Camp'. To my delight, the Cheshire Regiment were stationed there. In addition to entertaining the troops, we were also asked to do a show for the locals who had never in their lives seen a theatrical performance. A girl accordionist in our company managed to learn a local tune so that they could all join in.

On the night, we opened to great applause and ten minutes into the show the girl accordionist came on and played the local tune. The entire audience stood up and joined in the song which had about ten choruses — then, much to our amazement, as soon as it ended they all filed out of the hall! We quickly discovered that we had been playing their national anthem and they had been told that when the anthem was played, the show was over! Fortunately, the Military Police were on hand to explain things and bring them back in again.

Just before we left the islands, the whole company was invited to take tea with the Mayor. It was a very pleasant afternoon and we left on very amicable terms.

But it wasn't until we arrived at our next destination, Iceland, that we learned the awful truth. The day after we left, the very nice Mayor had been shot dead ... he was a German spy!

Life with ENSA had a comfortable sense of security about it. I was being paid a regular wage — I started on £6 5s a week, rising eventually by a pound or two as the war went on. Out of that we had to pay 35 shillings a week for accommodation, which was generally in ENSA hostels. As well as touring abroad, we also travelled to camps all over Britain — the Fleet Air Arm were our favourite audience as they were good listeners — and we always received tremendous hospitality. Of course, we never had to put our hands in our pockets for drinks after the shows as they were all bought for us.

Perhaps the most memorable visit was to the sealed camps on the Kent coast. We stayed at one camp near Dover just before the D-Day landings, and found ourselves right in the line of fire from the big gun in Calais.

Often in the middle of the show, the gunfire would start and the audience would gradually get smaller as they went to man the cross-fire and the noise would grow louder and louder with the cross-channel firing and the buzz bombs. I can remember spending my 21st birthday in Folkestone in Kent, too, and going to see my idols Laurel and Hardy at the local cinema while the buzz bombs flew over us.

Being with ENSA gave me the opportunity to do a bit of writing, too, and I actually wrote a screenplay called *War Blondes*. Teddy Harley who ran the Globetrotters was tremendously supportive and took it to somebody in the film world who was very interested. Unfortunately, the man died before it ever got any further, so my film writing career never got very far! The same fate befell a stage revue I wrote called *Without a Star*. A theatre impresario had expressed great interest, but that also vanished without a trace.

In addition to the scripts and screenplays that I wrote during my time in ENSA, I also wrote music and song lyrics. Many of them I can't remember, but I do recall a song I wrote for our visit to RAF camps, and which I often sing in our cruise talks as generally there are quite a few ex-service people among the passengers. It used to bring the house down in the RAF camps, and now it does on the cruise liners, too. It's called 'Pin-Up Boy':

I'm a pin-up boy
I'm the ladies' pride and joy
I'm the only thing that's left that's not in khaki
So for photographs I pose
Wearing a minimum of clothes
And I must confess my war job's rather parky
But if it helps to win the war
Just by standing in the raw
And being photographed just like a masculine cutie
For I have heard the sight
Of my photograph at night
Has helped the ATS to do their duty

I'm a pin-up boy
I'm the ladies' pride and joy
I'm the only boy that's not behind a propeller
Standing coyly in a plane
Wearing a little more than Jane
I could do with someone's aerial umbrella
I have given the WAAF the gen
On the magnificence of men
To her I'm just like Robert Taylor — only more so
And the snap to which she clings
Shows me with silver wings
And 'Per Ardua Ad Astra' on my torso

This third verse was for our visits to the Navy:

I'm a pin-up boy
I'm the ladies' pride and joy
They say Nelson lost his eye in admiration
Knowing just what sailors are
I am hung behind the bar
And peeps are rationed with discrimination
I've been pasted by the WRENS
On each telescopic lens
I'm the subject of eleven original shanties
And now the last battle's fought
The boys come home and I'll be caught
There'll be no future in appearing in my scanties!

I always say I really helped to win the war because, after the boys had seen my show, they couldn't wait to get out ... and get into battle!

It was quite a lesson in harsh reality to leave the comfortable cocoon of ENSA after the war, but I had a living to earn. I also had plans to get married.

Anne Rodgers, my fiancée, had been working in the Globetrotters on ENSA with me for three-and-a-half years and when the war was over I went to live with her family in Baron's Court in London. They had emigrated to England from New Zealand. Anne was an excellent singer and dancer and her family was full of very talented performers. Her father Percy ran a workmen's café, but her sister Thirza was an eminent ballerina and choreographer in Greatorex

Newman's Fol-de-Rols and her brother Barney was in a well-known adagio act (which involved extraordinary feats of balance), called Charles and Anita.

Anne and I shared a mutual love of showbusiness and had become close friends. But close friends we should have stayed. We married in 1948 because I suppose that, having had a strict upbringing, I, in my innocence, thought that under the circumstances we should make it official. I was 25 and Anne was a couple of years older than me.

However, there was no real romance between us and we realised that the whole thing was a mistake and so we got divorced after about two or three years — with no one else involved for either of us.

I went back to live in Chester but, after having been based in London, it was not very easy to get work from there.

* * *

Shortly before Anne and I were married, I found myself back entertaining the troops again. This time I was booked for a three-month tour around Germany and Austria for Combined Services Entertainment (CSE), the organisation that had replaced ENSA after the war. This was run by the War Office and provided entertainment for the many troops still left abroad.

In charge of the CSE at the time was Colonel Richard Stone, a man who was to play a very big part in my professional life. Well, certainly 10 per cent of it, for he went on to become one of the best-known agents in showbusiness and represented me for many years.

I was delighted to be back entertaining the troops and even more delighted at the chance of seeing some of the wonderful sights of the world.

One of the first tours I did was called *Ladies in Rhythm*, featuring the famous Ivy Benson Band — at the time without Ivy — the Beverley Twins and a marvellous ventriloquist called Jack Reed who was also from Chester and, funnily enough, had belonged to my original concert party there.

Our first eight weeks were spent in Germany. The girls in the band were a lively bunch and their names intrigued me because they reminded me of pirates. There was Alma Blow, Ivy Gunn, Bette Caddy and Ruby Costella — and they were conducted by a lady with the somewhat more mundane name of Betty Thomas. And some of their drinking capabilities would certainly outdo any pirate.

After a show, we were usually invited to the Officers' Mess for a drink. The young officers would swarm around the girls, plying them with booze and hoping to get them to throw their cares to the wind, as it were! But they had no such luck with the girls of the Ivy Benson Band. A sight imprinted on my memory is that of the officers legless under the table and the girls gaily drinking the night away.

It was at this time that I became a great fan of Danny Kaye. While in Hamburg, we were invited to his first performance in Europe for the troops. Unlike most orchestras who have their own musical director with whom to rehearse, Danny insisted on taking the rehearsal himself. He expected them to learn by his every movement or gesture with his fingers what he wanted them to do.

Musicians can be a hard bunch, and this lot were no exception, but after a session with Danny Kaye, they would come back terror-stricken by their perfectionist boss. However, on the opening night after the star had taken curtain call after curtain call, he finally turned to his band and said, 'You might think that I swore at you rather a lot, but, gentlemen, the greatest compliment I have ever been paid in my life is that I swore like an Englishman!'

Jack Reed, the Beverley Twins and I were also invited to see the European première of Danny's film *The Secret Life of Walter Mitty*. Jack, who was a hard drinker, had started particularly early that day. Half-way through the lunchtime showing, he disappeared. We assumed he had gone to the Gents, but he reappeared in the darkened cinema followed by a white-coated waiter carrying a tray of drinks. Jack made the poor man stand in the gangway for the whole of the film, filling up our glasses!

Among other things, Jack was my 'feed' in the show. One evening, we were due to leave the hotel for the theatre only to discover he had been missing all day. We eventually had a call to say he had been found lying in a gutter — literally — smashed out of his mind. Somehow, I managed to get him to the theatre, propping him up along the way as he vowed drunkenly, 'I'll never let you down.' And he was true to his word. He went on in front of an important audience and didn't miss a line or do anything wrong. But as soon as the curtain went down, he fell flat on his face! He was out cold as we took him back to the hotel to sleep it off and the rest of us headed for a local nightclub. At about 2.00am, in walked Jack ... raring to go again.

After Germany, Austria was our next port of call, where we arrived at Klagenfurt in the Tyrol. It was there I began to believe my home town truly seems to follow me everywhere for I suddenly received an unexpected call from a Mr CW Batey — my old headmaster at the King's School. He was working in Austria for UNESCO and invited me to go and have a drink with him. I was as nervous as the schoolboy I had been when I last saw him as I went along to face this ogre who had played such a big part in my formative years. But, of course, when I got there I discovered he was simply a man who liked having a social drink just as much as I did.

Trieste was our next stop on the way to entertain troops on the Yugoslav border. To this day, I will never forget the sight of a little man standing on a street corner, drenched to the skin and shaking his fist with rage.

Our coach had been held up in a square by rioting students who were not in the least perturbed by truncheon-waving policemen. Suddenly, a truck in front of us had its tarpaulin torn off to reveal a hose pipe which was aimed directly at the rioters. Within seconds of this camouflaged fire engine leaping into action, the square was completely cleared — with the exception of some innocent bystanders who had been watching the riot from a street corner. The little man was one of them and unfortunately he came off far worse than the rioters. But it just goes to show how violence can so easily be replaced by humiliation. There is no martyrdom in standing like a drowned rat as opposed to being able to boast of bruises and black eyes all gained in the efforts of your cause.

I have strong feelings for the causes I believe in and I'm proud to be British but there was one occasion working overseas when my loyalties were tested to the limit.

We had travelled to Egypt and were staying at the Grand Hotel Fayid in the canal zone. The hotel was a large, imposing building which was all on street level. On arriving from the airport, we were taken straight to the ballroom where dinner was being served and, much to our disgust, found that some stupid, drunken English officers had driven a sports car into the middle of the ballroom and were forcing the Egyptian waiters to push it out again. As I have said, I love my country, but at that moment I felt ashamed to be British.

This particular trip was certainly full of incidents. We were staying at Port Said and were due to travel to a place called Tel Akabir to do a show. Our route was down the Canal Road, which lay between the Suez Canal and the Sweetwater Canal. All heavy vehicles were supposed to take the Treaty Road beyond this.

The staff car we were travelling in was allowed to go along the Canal Road but the three-ton truck carrying all our costumes and luggage should have taken the other route. However, the driver reckoned it would be quicker to travel our way and, while he was driving along, realised his fuel tank was empty. Without stopping, he opened his driver's door to turn on a tap to release the emergency fuel tank — and promptly drove himself and all our props into the Sweetwater Canal! Needless to say, we weren't too amused at the time, but what we did find funny afterwards was that shortly before the accident two motorcycle policemen had spotted him in the distance and turned their bikes round to chase him for illegally driving along the Canal Road. Imagine their faces when they turned round ... and the truck had disappeared!

That night, we had to do the show in clothes borrowed from the officers but although our luggage was eventually rescued, with the exception of some of it that had been pilfered by locals who had jumped into the canal after it, it was totally unusable as anyone who falls in the Sweetwater Canal has to have at least 12 injections afterwards! This, of course, does not include the inhabitants who use the canal for literally everything ... including using it as drinking water. They would not touch the water we drank as they believed it had gone through the hands of the Devil.

The British seem to get into trouble whenever they are abroad. The beautiful island of Cyprus was no exception and I entertained the troops there several times in peace and in war.

The celebrated actor and writer Peter Jones was with me on one such tour when we had to be accompanied by bodyguards in bullet-proof cars because of the troubles. But, funnily enough, the only hostility we actually encountered was in a hotel in Larnaka where a Scotsman and a Yorkshireman started an argument about who had the superior country. It became so heated they broke the place up.

Peter himself became a little irate on this tour as we found we had been preceded by the antics of the Smith Brothers — a well-known act at the time — who had become quite famous on the island for their legendary drinking sprees. Peter was a moderate drinker who just enjoyed the odd glass of wine and became fed up with all the stories in the Officers' Mess about the wonderful Smith Brothers and their amazing capacity for drink. He felt that the tales were being aimed rather directly at his own modest intake. On the last night, he decided to dispel the myth that he was some sort of party pooper and got into a heavy drinking session with one of the top brass. At about 2.00am, the officer staggered off to bed, but Peter carried on and, after a couple of drinks, marched off to the man's room, knocked him up and made him get out of bed and start drinking again. Goodness knows how Peter felt in the morning, but I expect he thought it was worth it!

Everywhere we went around the camps, we were welcomed with open arms and royal hospitality. But performing one show in Germany, I experienced one of my most profoundly embarrassing moments.

We had arrived at the camp where we were being put up in the officers' very comfortable quarters and a bottle of champagne awaited us in the dressing room. Appearing in the show was a comedian and impressionist called Peter Kent. They were a great audience and laughed uproariously at everything.

Peter's act went down very well until he finished it with a very funny story about a man with a stutter. For the first time, there was complete silence at the end of the joke. We couldn't understand it.

We all went on stage at the end of the show so that the Group Captain could make his 'thank you' speech. To our sheer horror, he had the most pronounced stutter you had ever heard ... and our faces, especially Peter's, were turning redder by the moment!

Although he had had no idea about that particular situation, Peter was often a great practical joker himself. It was just before my birthday and we were doing a show in a different camp every night.

A week prior to my birthday, Peter announced in the Officers' Mess that it was my birthday that day. Of course, the drinks started flowing and we were up half the night. He did the same thing the next night at a different camp ... and the next, and by the time we got to my actual birthday we were both too ill to touch a drop!

On our CSE tours, we had an Escort Manager in each country. They always knew the area very well and used to show us around everywhere. In the Middle East, our Escort Manager was a wonderful Maltese character called Charlie Mazzola. He seemed to know everyone wherever we went, and we used to say that if he was to walk across the Sahara Desert, he would meet an Arab riding a camel who would say, 'Hello, Charlie.' He was a real Mr Fix-It and could arrange or obtain just about anything for you — from a new set of false teeth to a bottle of your favourite tipple. He escorted me on tours with people like Tony Hancock and Peter Jones and he was very popular with all the artistes.

Back in Britain in the mid-Fifties, I was having a lunchtime drink in my local pub in Regent's Park with actor Cardew Robinson. We were all set to go off that afternoon to see an all-ticket football match at Stamford Bridge between Chelsea and Arsenal. Suddenly, out of the blue, Charlie Mazzola appeared at the bar. He was paying a surprise visit to England, and we had had no idea he was in the country. He said he'd heard where we were and had decided to come and surprise us. We said unfortunately we couldn't stay long as we were going to the football match, so Charlie said that he would come over to Stamford Bridge with us. En route, we tried to explain that we had tickets for the match and that it would be difficult for him to join us. When we got to the ground, Cardew knew Ted Drake who was then the manager of Chelsea and he asked him if there were any spare tickets — but with no joy. 'Never mind,' said Charlie. 'I'll wait around and see you after the match.'

Feeling rather guilty, Cardew and I made our way to our seats in the stand. Then, about two minutes before the kick-off, we felt a tap on our shoulders. It was Charlie Mazzola! We couldn't believe our eyes. It turned out he'd met some bloke in a bar and managed to buy a ticket off him ... and got a seat right behind us! He really was one of the world's greatest Mr Fix-Its.

While I was working for the CSE, I was also making the odd television appearance back home. One of the shows I had started to get one-line parts in was *Hancock's Half Hour.*

I didn't know Tony Hancock well at this time but got to know him a bit better when he also came overseas to entertain the troops. We travelled all over the Middle East with a company that included Kenny Baker, Bette Smith (the well-known jazz singer) and Clifford Stanton.

We had finished off in Tripoli and Tony decided to stay on for a few days while the rest of us were flying to Malta to catch a connecting flight home.

Half-way through the flight, the pilot Captain Bethelson who had been ferrying us all over the place announced that Malta was fog-bound. He had enough fuel to get there and gamble on being able to land or he could turn around and go back to Tripoli. It was our decision.

It was rather a life-or-death moment, for if we had voted to go on to Malta we might have been unable to land and run out of fuel. So we decided the sensible thing to do was to return to Tripoli.

Tony Hancock was astonished to see us back. But it was not going to be the last time our paths were going to cross ... not by a long chalk.

It was just the beginning of a long friendship and working relationship which was going to launch me at last into the public eye.

4

Sun, Sea and Beauty Queens

There is nothing quite like a summer season or a seaside show. I've always loved the sea and in the days after the war these concert parties were highly popular in Britain's holiday resorts. As for me, well, I was in my element ... it's a paid summer holiday in a lovely resort with the sea and the sun providing an idyllic backdrop to work!

My début in summer seasons was in the year the war ended. We put on the *Gaiety Revels* at the Winter Gardens in Ventnor on the Isle of Wight. We were employed by a husband and wife team Will Tissington and Catherine Craig, who at one time ran a famous concert party called 'The Poppies'. By this time, I had taken to writing my own songs and this gave me the ideal opportunity to air my compositions. One of my songs featured in the show was called 'Holiday Sweetheart'. I used to sit on the side of the stage folornly with a sad and, I hoped, appealing expression and sing:

I don't mean to be funny but I don't want any money
I just want a Holiday Sweetheart
Someone within my reaches, to play with on the beaches,
I just want a Holiday Sweetheart ...

A three-line couplet followed and by then I like to think the audience had tears in their eyes! It didn't quite make the charts but it went down very well in Ventnor. In fact, the song became so successful that we even introduced a Holiday Sweetheart competition. Actually, the whole show was a huge hit with holidaymakers and locals alike and being young and full of enthusiasm we all became supreme optimists. So convinced were we that we could make a success of anything, the singer Charles Verity, the pianist Alan West and I decided to put on a show ... in the winter. So we hired the Town Hall in Ventnor for a week the following October. After all, we'd made friends with the locals and we were bound to pack them in. It lasted two nights. Nobody turned up! Undaunted, the following year saw me at the Devon resort of Babbacombe near Torquay where I was to appear for the following two years as well in summer season.

Again, I was employed by Tissington and Craig for a show called *Moonshine* and it was work I really looked forward to as the seasons ran for about 22 weeks so there would be no money worries over that period.

Unfortunately, my most vivid recollection of Babbacombe was losing my false teeth. I had been out on the Saturday night and had eaten some shellfish which violently disagreed with me the following day. On one of my urgent dashes to the loo, I inadvertently lost my dentures down the toilet bowl! Will Tissington couldn't see why I couldn't go on the following evening with no teeth ... but that's where I put my foot down.

Fortunately, the following day, a kind dental mechanic took pity on me and managed to knock me up a new set so that I was back on stage on the Monday night.

Lyme Regis in Dorset — now famous as the setting for the film *The French Lieutenant's Woman* — was another of my early venues for summer season.

The cast included Harold Berens, a wonderful dialect comedian, who was in the popular radio show *Ignorance is Bliss*; Peter Greenwell, who became the composer of many famous West End musicals; and Anthea Askey, whose father Arthur I met for the first time during that season.

The show used to be advertised on the sands by the town crier. While the show was running, my agent, Richard Stone, came down from London with a well-known pantomime producer Bert Montague who was interested in booking me and Harold for pantomime that year.

Apart from being a workaholic, Richard's other great love is sailing. So overjoyed was he at having left the hustle and bustle of London to visit Lyme Regis, and being overcome by the seascape, he decided it would be only sensible to combine business with pleasure. So he decided that the best way for us to negotiate the pantomime deal would be to hire a boat and take it out to sea.

However, Bert always looked the typical city gent. I never saw him dressed in anything but a full three-piece suit with overcoat and trilby hat. We must have looked a really incongruous sight — four men in a boat with Bert clutching at his trilby hat, being buffeted by the waves as we tried to negotiate contracts. Richard, however was enjoying himself so much that I had to tell him if we didn't start heading back for shore we would miss the first house. Usually strictly conscientious, Richard was so carried away by his idyllic surroundings that he replied it didn't matter at all.

We finally got back, if a little late, and also pulled off the pantomime deal. Financially, that summer season was not a very successful one and on the last night the sea came into Harold Berens's dressing room. We used to say it was the only thing that had come in all season!

Newquay in Cornwall became another resort which was to play a big part in my life. My first season there was in 1950 in a little venue called the New Theatre. This was owned by a delightful but rather eccentric lady called Miss Enid Hoskins who used to welcome patrons in the foyer wearing a long evening gown ... and carpet slippers! In the winter months, the New Theatre became a cinema showing feature films.

Miss Hoskins had a penchant for a well-known artiste at the time called Carl Ames, who appeared in her theatre billed as the 'international harpist'. He was a golden giant of a man — 6ft 5in and blond-haired. Miss Hoskins was so smitten with him that not only did she book him to appear in the summer seasons but in the winter she insisted on employing him to appear between the feature films, to do an act of about 15 minutes.

However, for the privilege of sitting close to her hero, Miss Hoskins decided to make the front row seats the most expensive in the house. It must have been the only cinema in the country where the film-goers had to pay more to crane their necks up at the screen!

Our summer show starred and was presented by George Lacy, probably the most brilliant dame comedian ever. It was an invaluable experience working with him, except when it came to our Sunday nights off.

George would invite the whole cast round to his digs. The only problem was that he would place one chair — his — in the centre of the room and we would all be expected to sit round and listen to his endless stories. There was plenty of food and drink provided, but that was just his way of ensuring he had a captive audience.

I got myself into a bit of girl trouble in Newquay when I dated a very tall girl called Val who was a hairdresser on holiday and staying in the same hotel as myself and my old mate from Chester, Jack Reid, who had joined the show. The hotel had given us specially reduced rates in return for the odd cabaret act and filling in as part-time barmen.

Val had told me she had a boyfriend back home in London who would be coming to join her but I thought I would worry about that when the time came.

One Saturday night, I was working behind the bar when

a very tall man — about a foot taller than Val — came in. I guessed correctly he was the boyfriend. After ordering a drink he started chatting and then confided in me that his girlfriend had seemed disinterested in him when he arrived and he suspected she was seeing someone else. He wondered if I might know who it was, as he'd like to put the mystery man through the nearest window! I think it must be at times like this when my slightly mad streak takes over, for I just looked at him and said, 'Yes, it's me.' The frankness of my admission seemed to stun him into complete silence. He sat there, looking slightly dazed, and had two more drinks before walking out of the bar, never to be seen again.

Although I was to return to Newquay at a later stage in a financial venture, I was to do many more summer seasons all over the country, especially at theatres on the end of piers. No stage in the world can compare with appearing on a pier. It's like running your own show from a desert island and no words can describe the feeling of performing in a theatre stuck out in the middle of the sea. And if your act doesn't go down well, you've always got the option of jumping over the side!

The Wellington Pier at Great Yarmouth is probably my most memorable seaside venue. It was there I made a life-long friendship and discovered that I was not destined to become a footballer. It was the mid-Sixties, at the height of the *Hugh and I* series, and Terry Scott and I were appearing at the theatre on the pier along with Donald Peers and the Dallas Boys.

I booked into the prestigious Carlton Hotel nearby and went into the bar for a large gin and tonic after my long drive there from London.

I was greeted by the owner, Kerry de Courcy, who is well known to many in showbusiness and we hit it off from the start. Well, actually within five minutes of meeting we started insulting each other, and to this day we are still exchanging insults. Kerry and his lovely wife Jean and their son James remain my closest friends. They have long since sold the Carlton but now own and run the superb Rye Lodge Hotel in the historic East Sussex town where I often visit them.

During our stay in Great Yarmouth, we were invited to get together a Showbiz XI football team to play a match against a local team for charity. Included in our team were Gerry and the Pacemakers and Dickie Henderson — and I was picked to play centre forward! I had heard somewhere that footballers often drank an egg beaten up in sherry to give them extra energy. So when the day of the great match dawned, instead of my usual lunchtime gin and tonic I decided to try that instead. The cocktail barman at the Carlton gladly provided me with my eggy sherry, and I was astonished to find that it tasted remarkably good. So I ended up having six! I have never had such energy in my life, and on the pitch I ran about like a man possessed. The only trouble was that by now I could barely see the ball. I even missed it when I went to take a penalty kick! So I think that heralded the end of my brief but memorable footballing career and, from then on, I have stuck to watching it on the telly from my armchair!

But it was on the world's longest pier that I learned an extra lesson about the timing of jokes. For if you appeared on

Southend Pier, you had no alternative but to time them properly.

I was appearing with my telly partner Terry Scott in a show called *Out of the Blue* and, much to our astonishment, we won the prestigious Outspan Award for the best summer show of its size — against all the odds.

The theatre at Southend was at the shore end of the pier and the distinct drawback was that it was directly over the station from which the pier train started. Apart from the usual intricacies of timing that we had to work out, we found ourselves having to allow for the trains arriving or departing to coincide with the punch lines! It didn't always work but it presented us with a marvellous excuse if we didn't get a laugh.

Half a suit hanging in my wardrobe always stirs memories of Bournemouth Pier. I appeared there several times, the most memorable being in the play *Birds of Paradise* with Peter Byrne of *Dixon of Dock Green* fame, Melissa Stribling and several beautiful girls. I was playing a drunken old major living on an island in the West Indies where I used to frequent the local House of Pleasure. The clients were invited to have their suits laundered while they were indulging in more pleasantly pressing pastimes! For the show, I had to have two panama suits, one which had to be very dirty with earth streaks on it, and the other a very smart replica of the first one which had supposedly been laundered at the brothel. The dirty suit was always very hot and sweaty after the performance and it took some explaining to the dry cleaners that it needed to be cleaned but have the dirty marks left on it. On stage, when I reappeared in my smart new suit, I had to fall down the stairs apparently from exhaustion! I became rather attached to my smart suit and at the end of the season asked the theatre manager Bertie Hare, the brother of Doris Hare, if I could buy it for a small fee and he agreed.

But on the very last night, when I fell down the stairs I managed to rip both knees. I've still got the suit ... but I can only wear the jacket.

I returned to Bournemouth some years later to do *Rattle of a Simple Man* with Ann Sydney, a local Bournemouth girl who had become the very first English Miss World. After that, Ann also joined me in a play called *Boeing Boeing* which opened there, and was a big success. The show went on to Blackpool Pier where we arrived with great optimism after our huge hit down South.

Outside the pier was a stall that sold the most delicious pancakes. As I passed it, the lady stall-holder called out to me, 'Hello, Hugh. We're all glad to know you're here for the season.' And she continued, 'What a cast! Dandy Nichols, Jimmy Thompson and Ann Sydney. But tell me, we've all been wondering — who is this group Boeing Boeing?'

That just about summed up the story of our flop at Blackpool. If the play had been called *Sex in the Skies* or *The Day the Pilot's Trousers Fell Down*, it would probably have been a great success. During the run, Ann had been hounded by the Press about a new love in her life. She eventually agreed to an interview and told them her new love was ... the theatre! This made all the headlines but one night when I was strolling along the pier with her she looked up at the very ordinary-looking theatre building and said, 'Who the hell could be in love with that?'

Of course, no entertainer's career could be considered complete at that time without a stint at Butlin's Holiday Camps. I did a couple of seasons at Pwllheli in North Wales where I was often asked to take part in judging their weekly Holiday Princess competitions. I soon discovered that if you were seen around the camp with a girl you fancied and she won the contest everybody accused the judges of favouritism. So the trick was to make sure the girl you were after came second or third — never first. That way, it stopped any accusations and also provided you with a great line in chat — 'Well, of course I voted for you — it was the other judges who have no idea of true beauty.'

But once, at Southsea Pier, I had to face a very angry audience who disagreed violently with the judges' decision. I was the main judge along with four others and the winner was a model who was a regular on the bathing beauty circuit and by far the most attractive competitor.

However, the audience all favoured a nurse who came second, because there were lots of her nursing colleagues in the audience. They booed and heckled the model who eventually lost her temper and stamped her foot and shook her fist at them, which incensed them even more! The management had a hell of a job getting the irate nurses out of the theatre and even more difficulty getting them off the end of the pier. Why, I don't know, but I ended up agreeing to try and pacify this crowd of wild women, and get rid of them. I can't remember exactly what I said, but somehow it worked and they left a little calmer.

The story made all the newspaper headlines the next day and it reminded me of the old saying that is engraved on the minds of most comedians: 'I don't mind them walking out during my act, but it's when they start walking towards me that I begin to worry!'

A season at Felixstowe in 1956 was probably one of the most important ones of my life. It was there I experienced two major changes in my life. I was to meet my second wife and I learned to drive! Josie Stewart, an accomplished pianist, was booked for the same season as me at the Spa Theatre. At the time, she was doing a very good double act on the piano with another girl, calling themselves Jill and Josie.

We were attracted to each other straight away and went out together throughout that 16-week period. We both knew we were destined to marry but we couldn't straight away for, although by now I was divorced from my first wife Anne, Josie was only separated from her first husband and obviously we had to wait for her divorce to come through before we could get married.

Unbeknown to me, Josie was suffering agonies over a closely guarded secret all through those weeks, and could not bring herself to confide in me. Eventually, her partner Jill was instructed to reveal this terrible skeleton in my future wife's closet. I waited with some trepidation as Jill revealed ... that Josie's name wasn't Josie at all — it was Mavis Lillian Polley! Well, it didn't put me off and we married in the late Fifties. But that was around the time that I started to become well known with the Hancock TV shows and later, of course, *Hugh and I.*

It was over this course of time that I discovered fame is a great magnet for some ladies and a lot of temptation was thrown my way.

Work kept me away from Josie a great deal and I did tend to enjoy myself but with my puritan upbringing it also brought a feeling of shame and I started to feel guilty whenever I was with my wife. Also, the fact that we lived in a lovely sixteenth-century cottage in Cobham, Surrey, didn't help. Josie loved it — but I hated it.

It was very isolated and surrounded by trees and I felt claustrophobic and hemmed in, as I enjoy looking out over a wide open view, such as the one I have now, overlooking a vast expanse of ocean, which is wonderful.

We had a couple of burglaries which didn't help my lack of enthusiasm about the place, either. At the time, we had a golden labrador dog called Oliver and one night Josie and I awoke to find someone in our bedroom with a torch. I gave a yell and tentatively chased the intruder downstairs — following at a safe distance, I must admit! However, he got away, although he was caught later by the police, but I couldn't understand why there hadn't been a peep out of Oliver. Then I went into the kitchen and discovered that the burglar had got out the same way as he had broken in — through the window and over my sleeping dog! I went mad with him and when the police arrived shortly afterwards, his hackles went up, he bared his teeth, and he wouldn't let them through the door!

On another occasion, my mother had come from Chester to stay with us so that she and Josie could come to see Terry and me performing in Southsea.

When we got home, we found we had been broken into again! My mother found it all quite exciting — things like that didn't happen in Chester. But the burglar had taken quite a bit — some valuable cutlery and jewellery and all sorts of other things.

Amazingly, we got some of it back because the police discovered it was someone like a local milkman who was just doing it for the excitement. So he hadn't sold a lot of it on, and just kept it at home where the police discovered it.

However, it was the kind of excitement I could well do without and I didn't want to have to worry about the house all the time when we were both away working.

All in all, what with the separations and one thing and another, Josie and I decided to part in the late Sixties, having been married for 12 years.

It was all very amicable, and I went to live in a flat in Maida Vale.

Josie still lives in the same cottage to this day and occasionally we are in touch and exchange Christmas cards.

So Felixstowe was a pretty memorable place for me, because not only did I meet Josie but at that time I had always wanted to drive. Until then, I had never been able to afford even a modest car. Now I was 35 and decided it was high time I took lessons.

I still remember the first words my driving instructor said. As I switched on the engine, he said, 'You are now able to kill.' Chilling, but effective.

I took my test in the lunch hour at nearby Ipswich and

was pleased that the countryside there is very flat. What I hadn't counted on, however, was that being lunch-time all the employees of the surrounding offices and factories were leaving the buildings for their meal break ... on bicycles! There were cyclists everywhere, but fortunately I managed not to run any down and passed first time. Sadly, now the days of the summer seasons are over. Variety shows and concert parties are a thing of the past, and I think it's a terrible shame.

They were a wonderful training ground for many an entertainer, dancer, singer and musician and produced some of the finest names in showbusiness today. But nowadays, of course, the seaside theatres won't take the gamble of running a summer show for so many weeks, preferring instead to have one-nighters with pop groups or singers or the odd comedian.

I had a ball during my run of summer seasons — although, of course, they were hard work as well.

After appearing in countless shows, I became involved in a financial venture in Newquay where I joined up with husband-and-wife team Ronnie Brandon and Dickie Pounds, who were responsible for discovering not only Terry Scott and myself but the likes of Bruce Forsyth, Roy Hudd and Felix Bowness.

We put on a highly successful Old-Time Music Hall. At the start, I was a sleeping partner but I used to go along to the shows each season to watch the acts.

Eventually, I became Chairman of the show and also got more involved with the financial side of the business, thanks to coaching from Dickie who produced the show as well as being a wizard with figures.

As Chairman, I could see for the first time the faces of the audience from the wings, when they couldn't see me. It always amazes me how so many people who don't seem to react by laughing out loudly are, in fact, enjoying it inwardly and it shows on their faces. If only they realised how much that means to a performer.

This was also apparent to my little dog at the time — a dachshund called Tekel.

One of my songs that closed the show was 'Will She be Waiting Up?'. It was a very poignant number and gave the audience the impression I was singing wistfully about my wife. However, in the last line it became apparent I was, in fact, singing about my pet dog. At that point, Tekel would run on to the stage, jump on to my lap and lick my face — partly out of affection, but mostly because she loved the taste of grease-paint! This, of course, would bring 'oohs' and 'aahs' and applause from the audience and Tekel absolutely revelled in the limelight.

But one night we were faced with the most unresponsive audience ever. Throughout the show, nothing could move them and we tried our hardest, in vain, to get a laugh out of them.

So when Tekel pranced on stage as usual, much to her astonishment there was no enthusiastic murmuring, no applause. Just the stony-faced audience we'd had all evening.

Tekel jumped on to my lap as usual but, instead of licking me, just turned towards the audience, looked them over and gave an enormous yawn!

Newquay is also memorable as being the venue for my very first summer season with Terry Scott. It was the forerunner to four consecutive seasons I would play with Terry and we worked well together from the start.

Little did either of us dream it would also be the forerunner to a smash-hit television series which would run for 79 episodes over six years and bring us both instant stardom.

5

I Ran Away with Hancock's Wine Gums!

Wherever I go, in this country or overseas, I am inevitably asked the same question over and over again — 'What was he really like?' He, of course, was Tony Hancock, probably one of the greatest comedy actors we have ever witnessed. And for several years, I shared a close friendship and working relationship with him.

My first appearance in *Hancock's Half Hour* on BBC TV was in November 1957 when I played the first son in 'The Adopted Family', in which Tony had to produce a wife and four children to get to the top of the list for a council house. He adopts Sid James and four of his mates and then finds he can't get rid of them.

It was probably only one or two lines but it was the

beginning of many regular appearances on the show.

Overall, I played the most extraordinary range of characters: Clerk of the Court, Last Man, First TV Repair Man, a Sergeant, Tree Inspector, First Old Man, Librarian (twice), a Disbeliever, the Usher, Railway Ticket Clerk, Ship's Steward, Launderette Attendant, Secretary, Turnstile Attendant, Smudger Smith, Bert, Photographer's Assistant, Second Councillor, Florist, Liftman and Blood Patient ... of course, from the legendary 'Blood Donor' sketch.

I came to know Tony well in the early days of the show because we travelled together overseas entertaining the troops in Malta, Tripoli and Cyprus. I came to know his obscure philosophies on life and his drinking habits. Accompanying us were the jazz singer Betty Smith and her husband Jack Peberdy, Clifford Stanton (who was a distinguished cabaret act) and trumpeter Kenny Baker. Cicely, Tony's wife, was with us, too, and I can remember that he seemed very happy then. Certainly some of my happiest memories of Tony are of that time.

Tony performed three acts — the first was a juggling act, the second the readings of Charles Dickens and finally his great crooner's skit. I acted as his footman/dresser in one act and was his pianist in the latter, as well as doing my own act.

After the show, we were always entertained by the officers in the Mess. But if they started to tell jokes and expected Tony to start telling gags, too, he wanted to leave very quickly because he didn't like that at all. In private, he just wasn't a funny man — he wasn't an extrovert. He'd rather curl up under a stone.

If, however, there were perhaps two or three officers who wanted to talk about politics or obscure religions then Tony was happy to stay all night as long as the vodka was flowing. On one occasion, we did a show on the *Ark Royal* in Malta and were entertained in the ward-room afterwards until the early hours.

Immediately after the overseas tours, I started to get better parts in *Hancock* than the one-liners I had had before. Tony and I had become good friends by now and he used to come back to my one-room flat in Regent's Park to play Pic-a-Stic, a game he adored. It was the most unlikely game for him as the one thing you need is a steady hand which Tony certainly didn't have, but the fact that he couldn't do it, resulting in sticks falling down in cascades all over the place, made him hysterical with laughter. He had a simple mind about things like that. He had this habit of throwing his head back when he laughed and I remember once he was sitting on the floor and laughing so much at something that he kept hitting his head on the light switch. We suggested that he moved his position but he refused, saying he was enjoying it too much.

Working with Hancock was a jolt to the system for any actor who works to a reasonably disciplined regime. *Hancock's Half Hour* was filmed on a Friday and usually we wouldn't start being word-perfect until mid-week. But Tony, who had a terrible memory, was different. By the weekend prior to filming, he'd learned the entire script. On the Tuesday at rehearsal he would be absolutely brilliant; in fact, it's the only time I've ever known an actor applauded by the rest of the cast at rehearsals.

But then on the Wednesday morning he would come in and say to Duncan Wood, the producer, 'I'm not sure if I'm going to remember that scene.' And then the rot would set in. The following day it would get worse and he would forget something else. By Friday they had to set up cues or hide lines on the soles of people's shoes! If we were filming outside, say in a garden, he'd have his lines stuck in flower bushes or on nearby trees.

In one programme, 'The Oak Tree', Hancock's pride and joy, an oak tree in his garden, is threatened with removal and he organises a protest march and a local demo to try and save it. I was playing the Trees Inspector, and little Johnny Vyvyan (who was in most of the *Hancock's Half Hours*) played a marcher. Johnny had to put his foot on a table to show how the sole of his shoe was worn out from marching, and there on the sole was chalked Tony's next line! Tony was absolutely doubled up with laughter when he saw it.

But though he could see the funny side of his obsession with forgetting his lines, nothing seemed to cure him of it. He suffered terrible doubts and I've never known an actor as nervous before doing a show. Every muscle in his face would twitch and he would rather die than start.

Someone else who suffered a similar anguish during live filming was the legendary comedian Tommy Trinder. Lovely actress and friend Pat Coombs and I signed up to do an eight-week television series with the great man. Unfortunately, we ended up only doing two weeks of it, although we did get paid for the whole series. The reason for this is that Tommy — whose catchphrase 'you lucky people' was known nationwide — was so wonderful at doing warm-ups for the studio audience before the show. He did all his own warm-ups and was quite brilliant at them — he had the audience rolling in the aisles. But when it came to the actual show, he just couldn't cope with the discipline of the sketches and the cameras and was, all in all, pretty useless. Subsequently, the show wasn't very good, and the BBC pulled the plug on it after just a fortnight. Still, we got our money — but it would have been nice to have done the full eight weeks.

And that wasn't my only experience of well-known entertainers suddenly coming up with something wholly unpredictable — and sometimes at the most inappropriate time! Larger-than-life comedian Fred Emney used to run his own big revue shows in the West End. He and his two sisters used to send their mother £1 a week each towards her upkeep. But his sister Joan — who was known, for some strange reason, as Joan Fred Emney — was not quite as reliable and regular in her contributions as her siblings. In one of Fred's shows, he had a marvellous first entrance — the stage was set out like the Alps and Fred used to emerge dressed as usual in top hat, evening cloak and tails, wearing a monocle and smoking a large cigar. He would make his way across the stage and say to an 'Alpine Guide' who was already positioned there, 'Have you seen a big fat man wearing a top hat, tails and an evening cloak and smoking a big cigar?' And the Alpine Guide would reply, 'No,' to which Fred Emney retorted, 'Good God, I'm lost!'

One matinée, Fred made this wonderful entrance as usual but, before the Alpine Guide had had a chance to utter his 'No', Fred suddenly spotted his sister Joan sitting in the front row. Instead of carrying on with his 'Good God, I'm lost!' line, Fred strode to the footlights, leaned over and shouted loudly to Joan, 'Where's Mother's pound?'

When I appeared with Fred in JB Priestley's *When We Are Married*, most of the cast — including myself, Peggy Mount and Frank Thornton — used to make an entrance on stage together and we always got a good entrance round (applause) from the audience. But Fred made his appearance on his own. More often than not, he would get an entrance round as well, but sometimes he didn't. And if he didn't, he would sulk for the rest of the show!

When he came on, he was supposed to have a short conversation with the maid who says to him, 'Are you married?' to which Fred was supposed to reply, 'No.' On one occasion, he didn't get the entrance round so he was sulking, and instead of answering 'No' when asked if he was married, he replied, 'Yes' instead. There was a long awkward silence for about two minutes, and the poor girl playing the maid hadn't a clue what to do. After a while of this silent torture, Fred gave in and said, 'Oh, all right then, no.' He really was a one-off.

On the other side of the coin, I was appearing in the show *Boeing Boeing* on Blackpool Pier with Dandy Nichols and Jimmy Thompson, as well as the first British Miss World Ann Sydney, who had by then gone into showbusiness. Dandy, Jimmy and I always got a round of applause when we first came on, but the others in the cast who were not so well known usually didn't. One night, Ann Sydney made her entrance and there was one solitary clap from the audience. Ann stood still, forgot her lines and just said, 'It's me mum!' And it was!

To return to Hancock, of course the 'Blood Donor' sketch is probably the most famous of all the television *Hancock's Half Hours*. I played the man in the next bed conversing with Tony who offers me a wine gum — 'Don't take the black one' — and I end up walking off with the whole packet. That sketch has become a legend to Hancock fans but few know the real story behind it.

Shortly before doing the 'Blood Donor', Tony and Cicely had a minor road accident which threw him so much he insisted on the whole show being done on autocue. In my scene with him, we just lay in the beds next to each other reading our lines from the prompt.

I appeared in two Hancock films — *The Rebel* and *The Punch and Judy Man*. In the former, I just had a one-line part as a train passenger, but in the latter I had a much bigger role as Hancock's fellow Punch and Judy Man.

We shot the film in Bognor Regis on the Sussex coast where at one point we drank the town out of vodka. On the first night we checked into a local hotel on the seafront and I went up to my room to have a bath before going downstairs to meet the others for a drink in the bar. When I turned the taps on, nothing happened. I assumed there must have been something wrong with the water system and decided to go for a drink.

Chatting away, I forgot all my intentions of having a bath, and a little while later there was a tremendous crash in the restaurant. Everybody dashed in to see what had happened and discovered that part of the ceiling had caved in. The culprit? Me!

While I had been down in the bar drinking, the water — which for some unknown reason had been temporarily cut off — had come on again. I hadn't switched the taps off properly after trying them and the bath had overflowed. The management were very good and assured me it wasn't my fault as there had been no warning about the water being off and actually they were very pleased as they told me they could get a brand-new ceiling on the insurance!

One of the cast, who was also a regular in the *Half Hour*, was a marvellous, warm-hearted Italian called Mario Fabrizi. He was a wonderful character, a bit like Sam Costa. He was supposed to be an Italian Count or something and he loved the good life in every way, and Tony adored him. Mario was a great puller of women. He used to sit in the hotel looking out over the seafront and one of the cast only had to remark on an attractive girl passing by and within minutes Mario had dashed outside and never failed to bring the particular lady back.

Some of the *Punch and Judy Man* scenes were filmed at Elstree Studios in Hertfordshire. One morning, Mario, John Le Mesurier and I were doing a scene in which we were waiting for Tony to join us in a local pub. We started shooting at around 8.00am. John and I were given pints of ordinary beer to drink, but Mario insisted on having bottles of Green Shield Worthington, which was pretty potent stuff.

Every time we shot a take, John and I would just take a

sip from our glasses, but Mario would knock back the whole bottle and demand another one. The trouble was that the scene took about twelve takes.

By the time it came to Tony's entrance, Mario had fallen off his bar stool and had passed out drunk on the floor! Of course, filming had to be abandoned for the rest of the day but Tony wasn't in the least bit annoyed. Far from it. He thought the whole episode was hysterically funny.

He was also reduced to crying with laughter when we shot 'The Missing Page', in which I played the librarian. Two great old character actors, Gibb McLaughlin and Kenneth Kove, were doing a scene in which Gibb had the line: 'Don't you shush me, Frobisher — it's this ruffian here,' pointing to Tony.

Poor old Gibb just couldn't get the name Frobisher right while rehearsing it. He'd say 'Froshibar ... Frobesheer ...' anything but the correct name. But when it came to the take, he actually managed to pronounce it correctly — but on his second line he pointed to Tony and said, 'It's this Russian here.' Tony just fell on the floor weeping with laughter.

John Le Mesurier was a lovely character, too, if a trifle absent-minded at times. One evening, he came back to the hotel in a terrible state. He'd parked his car somewhere and totally forgotten where he'd left it. We all set off to scour the back-streets of Bognor to search for it, but in the end returned to the hotel having drawn a blank. As we approached the hotel John just stopped in his tracks. There, parked right outside the hotel, was his car ... where it had been all along.

Filming is usually a long, arduous day with a very early start and a lot of hanging about and we didn't usually finish until about 8.30pm when the cast and crew all liked to go for a couple of drinks and something to eat. But Tony used to like to go on drinking for as long as possible and, frequently, in the make-up room at the crack of dawn the next morning, he'd be shaking so much he would say that the only thing for it was to have another vodka. And he would.

Having said that, most of the time I knew Tony I remember there being a lot of happiness and certainly lots of laughter. At that time, the vodka had not taken a complete grip on him.

When Tony was sober, he was a very pleasant type of chap but when he'd had a few he could be quite rude to his fans. I remember we were in a bar once and a fan called out, 'Have a drink on me, Tony.'

Tony replied that he'd have a large vodka and tonic.

One of the group we were with said it wasn't fair to ask for a large one when they'd been good enough to offer him a drink in the first place, but Tony answered, 'If people want to buy me a drink then they can buy me what I want.'

By now, Josie and I had moved to our very isolated country cottage in Cobham in Surrey. We were miles from anywhere, although the local pub, The Black Swan, was run by Bill and Maud Lamb who are now close neighbours of mine in Sussex.

Tony, by now, had moved in not far from us and he used to invite Josie and me to lunch on Sundays to his house in Blindley Heath which was called McConkeys. If we decided not to drive home, we would have to stay at a local hotel as it was impossible to stay at Tony and Cicely's. They had only furnished their bedroom and the downstairs lounge and kitchen, so no one could ever stay there because there was nothing in the other bedrooms at all. It was a big house but I don't remember them ever getting round to putting up curtains. The bar was firmly in place, though, and on those Sundays we'd gather round it at about noon for a drink before lunch. The drinks would be flowing and, at about 2.30pm, Cicely, who was a very good cook, would announce that lunch was ready. But Tony was never ready to sit down and eat, so the drinking would go on until about 5.00pm by which time nobody really wanted to eat —and the lunch was usually ruined.

Cicely was a wonderful wife to him and tried very hard in the early days to curtail his drinking habits but, sadly, in the end because she loved him so much, she joined him.

I was becoming quite well known in my own right by then, a situation that was responsible eventually for the cooling off of our friendship.

The Westminster Bank staff magazine voted me their TV Character of the Year, awarding me an imaginary Oscar. They said I had popped up so often on the television screen, lumped in with several credits after 'and' and 'with', that they had taken to shouting, 'Oh look ... there he is again!' and they didn't even know my name! But I think the change came over Tony when he did a *Face to Face* interview with presenter John Freeman. He was very nervous doing the interview but he got a lot of public praise for it and he suddenly began to believe that he was an important figure, not for what he did in comedy but for his thinking. He started to regard himself as a superior statesman, a philosopher. And from that day on, there seemed to me to be a slight shift in his attitude towards everything.

He did have a lot of control over his television programmes but he needed the discipline of directors and writers and I think he felt he had risen above all that and could do it on his own. But there is no great artiste who doesn't need somebody to be an intermediary between them and the public eye. It's got to be channelled with an outside eye rather than your own. Quite a lot is done on instinct, but there wasn't so much instinct with Tony really, he worked really hard at his comedy.

He cooled off towards people who understandably wanted to go their own way at some point. It was a shame, really, because I experienced later on what many of the people, such as Sid James, who had been associated with him earlier, experienced. We had been such close friends, but when I went into my own series, *Hugh and I*, there was a sort of rejection on his part.

I only saw him about twice after that — he wasn't rude, just distant. He was no longer the warm-hearted person I used to know. I think he just wanted people to be permanently part of his team. I don't know if any sort of envy was involved in it, but he just seemed to lose all interest in you as a person.

Of course, I have a lot to thank *Hancock's Half Hour* for. It made my face well known on the screen, and today I am still getting royalties from the sales of videos and cassettes. Not bad for a job I did more than 40 years ago!

I think the reason why Hancock is so popular today is that he was a sort of lower/upper-class rebel. The hurt dignity and the frustration at having petty officials bossing him about ... that is what he portrayed.

The difference between the kind of scripts which were written at that time and most of today's modern sitcoms is that the former told a story — they had a beginning, a middle and an end and left you with a feeling of satisfaction. You weren't left wondering what on earth happened. Of course, there are some very good sitcoms today but many are absolute rubbish.

I was in pantomime in Manchester when I heard about Tony's suicide in Australia. I was obviously upset but I wasn't surprised because some time earlier I had done a television series in Australia with that prolific comedy writer David Croft and I saw the rushes of the start of a sitcom Tony had done there. It was so amateurish compared with all the things he had done for the BBC. But I couldn't feel an enormous sense of loss over his death because he had virtually cut himself off. Even when he was alive, he had cut himself off from friends.

Was he a genius? I don't know the answer to that one. He had a style all his own and, great though the scripts were by Ray Galton and Alan Simpson, I can't think of anyone who could have done them better.

Tony was always searching for something. I don't know if he really knew what for. He wanted the answer to whether there is life after death. That was very important to him and it is strange that his quest for the answer has been given after his own death — it is obvious to everybody that Hancock lives on.

I have never worked before or since with a character like Tony Hancock. He was a one-off — unique. And however much people may criticise his temperament and his drinking, I just treasure the happy memories I have of a good friend. After all, he left us one of life's most precious gifts ... a legacy of laughter.

6

Hugh and I

From the very beginning, Terry Scott and I could never agree on how to say 'Hugh and I'. I always put the emphasis on the 'Hugh', while Terry put it on the 'I'.

It was a television series created for two unknowns that was to lead to something beyond our wildest dreams. Although in personality we were often like chalk and cheese, as a team we worked very well together.

One of my favourite descriptions of us is 'The Whisky and the Ginger' — Terry being the effervescent mixer and myself the stimulant! The programme made us household names and in the five years it ran we made two very special fans ... Her Majesty the Queen and Sophia Loren.

Terry and I first met in Weymouth in 1953 when we

were booked to appear there for a variety week with Morton Fraser's Harmonica Band topping the bill. I shared digs with Terry and his first wife Thelma and I can remember we just couldn't stop laughing all that week.

The next year saw us booked at the New Theatre in Newquay, Cornwall, where we did a revue called *Into the Sun*, as well as my own act entitled *Fun in Gloom*.

Terry and I did some sketches together — 'The Fire Brigade', along with my old mate Jack Reed; 'Courting Disaster' with Erica Yorke in which I played the fiancé and Terry played the little boy; and 'Home Comforts' with Peggy Barret in which Terry and I both played the lodgers ... a role I was to play for several years in *Hugh and I*.

The revue was devised by Peter Croft, who was later to become the producer of *Crossroads*, and Richard Stone who represented both of us as our agent at the time.

In the programme, I was described as finding it 'difficult to smile but confesses his maximum temptation to do so is at the charming scenery (feminine) of Newquay'. It was Terry, though, who got into trouble with his philandering this time round. He and Thelma were married but he still self-confessedly had an eye for the ladies and made a date with one of the dancers in the show to meet her outside the local picture house. It was blinding sunshine when they went into the darkened cinema and, after they had settled in their seats, Terry, not wanting to waste any time, suggested they moved to the back row.

Groping their way in the pitch-black they sat down and, delighted with his success so far, Terry put his arm around the girl ... or so he thought, until a gruff male voice came out of the darkness, 'I think you've got the wrong person, mate!'

While we were performing at Newquay, summer season producers Ronnie Brandon and Dickie Pounds came to see us and promptly booked us for three consecutive seasons at Southend, Felixstowe and Hastings.

Prior to arriving at Felixstowe, I rented a flat for myself and Terry for around £10 a week. At the end of the first week, I put my £5 on the table as my share but Terry wasn't having it. He wanted me to pay £4.50 or whatever it was pre-decimalisation, so that he could pay the difference and in doing so tell everybody it was *his* flat. A similar thing happened over all our payments for television and theatre acts.

We were paid, for some reason, in thirteenths and Terry insisted on getting seven-thirteenths while I only got six. The reason? So that he could claim he was the leading role in the act.

If it had been a vast difference, of course, I would have objected, but the whole thing was so trivial and stupid I just couldn't be bothered.

That was Terry all over. But in spite of petty differences we were a great working team and in the main got on well together.

One year we did summer season at Weston-super-Mare and proved a great attraction as the first series of *Hugh and I* had just been screened.

By the end of the first week we had broken all theatre records and bought champagne for the rest of the company.

Terry, in his own inimitable style, announced that if we did the same the following week we would buy champagne again. Well, he was rather hoisted by his own petard as we broke box office records again the next week, and for the following three weeks, by which time Terry was desperately running round Weston-super-Mare trying to find the cheapest champagne.

On the last night of the season at Weston, lots of farewells and thank you speeches were to be made — one by the Entertainments Manager who happened to be the local Mayor that year and one by Terry and myself. We decided that we would each make a speech, Terry thanking half the people and me the other half. However, on the night Terry got carried away and rambled on thanking anything and everybody — leaving me with nobody left to thank! There was only one thing to do. My oration was one line: 'I think Weston's got a super Mayor.' It brought the house down.

I have always believed in keeping things short and to the point as it makes far more of an impact than going all round the houses.

While we were doing our summer seasons, I was making a name for myself in *Hancock's Half Hour* and had also made several appearances during 1955–56 in *Great Scott — It's Maynard*, along with Terry, Bill Maynard and that wonderful comedy actress Pat Coombs, who to this day remains a good friend.

Duncan Wood, who was in charge of situation comedy at the BBC, produced the series and also came along to see Terry and me in summer season. The BBC was looking for a

Laurel and Hardy-type team for a new comedy venture. At the time, I was thin and Terry was, well, fatter than me. (After that, we gradually grew to be about the same size!) The local papers that had reviewed our summer season acts described us as 'droll' and 'lugubrious' and Duncan got the idea of teaming us up for the proposed new TV series.

The powers that be at the Beeb also seemed to think that we were an ideal combination. And so *Hugh and I* was born ... and soon it was being hailed by the critics as a sort of comedy *Coronation Street*. Of course, it meant instant stardom and public recognition for myself and Terry, as I became all too aware of very quickly.

And in terms of public recognition, it always amuses me how some people need to surround themselves with famous people. At one time, I was holidaying in Cap d'Antibes on the French Riviera. We were staying at a lovely hotel called Hôtel La Bouée on Plage de la Garoupe, situated on its own private beach. While staying there, we met a charming couple from Yorkshire who had a large jewellery business back home. They were lovely company but rather inclined to be big name-droppers — indeed, they did know quite a lot of well-known people, including Pools owner Robert Sangster whom we met while we were staying there.

One day, we paid a visit to the perfume centre of Grasse and we were all walking along the high street when suddenly a large bellow came from the other side of the road, 'Hello, Hughie!' And then a large figure strode towards us. It was the Marquess of Bath who knew me well because he had been to see Terry and me in summer season at Weston-super-Mare and we had opened some caves for him. (In fact, I still have a Punch's head on a stick at home inscribed with the words: Presented to Hugh Lloyd by the Marquess of Bath, 28th July 1963'.) After a little chat, he moved on.

'Who was that?' asked our name-dropping friends.

'Oh, just the Marquess of Bath,' I replied smugly ... leaving them for once speechless and open-mouthed. They didn't drop too many names after that.

And on the subject of fame, it's easy for one's ego to become completely overblown when faced with such glowing public endorsements as that which appeared in the *Observer* magazine in the late Sixties. The magazine ran a feature on who would be President of England should the Royal Family be deposed. They went through the ranks of various professions to bring out various names to be considered. As far as I can remember, Peter Ustinov was one of two from the theatrical profession to be named and, for some reason, I was the other! It might have been because during the three previous years I had been President of the Concert Artistes' Association ... I just don't know. One thing I do know for certain is that if I were made President, the first thing I would do would be to ban garlic in public places!

While I was rehearsing for the first series of *Hugh and I*, my wife Josie was appearing in summer season at the Lido Theatre in Margate with comic Jimmy Wheeler. As I was staying down at the Kent seaside resort with her, I decided to commute to town every day. I prefer to call commuters 'computers' because the stony-faced, pin-stripe-suited gentlemen who look as if they are permanently glued to the seats of the first-class compartments of the 8.35 seem as though they can only be operated by pressing a 'motivate' button.

I had a first-class weekly season ticket and must have stuck out like a sore thumb wearing my actor's gear of T-shirt and casual trousers and reading my *Daily Mirror*. I stood out like a bible in a bookmakers amidst that sea of *Guardians* and *Financial Times*. And I felt like a real interloper, for wherever I seemed to sit I got the distinct feeling, judging by the frosty looks from my fellow travellers, that I was sitting in George's seat, or Henry's or Norman's. However, just before *Hugh and I* was transmitted for the first time, the *Radio Times* did a big feature on Terry and me and our pictures were on the front cover. One of my fellow 'computers' obviously read the magazine and my presence the day after it came out was greeted with a totally different reaction. The *Radio Times* had been passed around the compartment and there was obviously a great deal of relief at discovering the identity of this strange chappie who had been occupying their sacred seats. And from that moment on, I became accepted as a member of the First Class Commuters' Club!

Hugh and I was based around 33 Lobelia Avenue, Tooting, where Terry lived with his mother (played by Vi Stevens) and I was the lodger and the only one bringing any money into the household from my job in a factory.

Terry played a rather hopeless bachelor who dreams of aspiring to wealth without having to work and is continually dreaming up ridiculous schemes to achieve it. As the gullible lodger, I was led by him into one adventure after another, but

I was usually the one who got the girl in the end. In fact, my screen girlfriend, who lived next door, was played first by Jill Curzon and then by *EastEnders* star Wendy Richard.

The next-door neighbours were the Wormolds, played by Patricia Hayes and Cyril Smith (and, in a later series, Jack Haig) and the Crispins, whose roles were taken by the marvellous Mollie Sugden and Wallas Eaton, his part being taken over later by Charles Dyer, who wrote the plays *Rattle of a Simple Man* and *The Staircase.*

Only one thing was missing from the cosy set-up, decided the scriptwriters, and that was a dog. So one day, Terry went out and got a lovely spaniel called Tricia who he kept as a pet and who was to remain with us throughout the five-year series. Tricia got so used to the set as a second home that if anyone knocked on the door she would need no encouragement to bark. She got so good at learning what to do that instead of having to bring her into rehearsals as originally intended she needed only to arrive in the studio on the day of recording.

Hugh and I was written by John Chapman, a wonderful character with a great sense of humour. He had previously been involved in writing some screened one-off farces for Brian Rix and seemed the ideal man for the job — which he was — as he was only interested in writing comedy, unlike some other comedy writers of that time who felt that they had to get a sort of message across in their scripts. The producer was David Croft who has given his tremendous enthusiasm and technical qualities to countless other comedy series like *Dad's Army*, *'Allo 'Allo*, *Hi-de-Hi* and *You Rang, M'Lord.*

Hugh and I

Off screen, Terry and I shared a lot of laughs. Our working commitments meant we spent a lot of time together, although socially we certainly didn't live in each other's pockets. We only lived a few miles apart in Surrey — Josie and myself in Cobham and Terry, who was divorced from Thelma by this time, now lived with his new wife Maggie in Wormley, near Guildford.

On one occasion, our working partnership even extended to us sharing an audition together! In the late 1960s, Otto Preminger, the famous Hollywood film director came to Britain to direct Laurence Olivier in the film *Bunny Lake Is Missing*. He wanted for the smaller parts some well-known British TV faces. Terry and I were sent along to the audition. When we arrived, we were shown into a room with about 20 of the best-known faces on television in it! When it came to our turn — with everyone else having gone in individually — Terry and I went in together. To Otto Preminger's surprise, his secretary announced, 'Terry Scott and Hugh Lloyd.'

The 'great' man was sitting at a desk flanked by his inscrutable henchmen and there was just one chair opposite him at the desk, which Terry, of course, immediately occupied. The only chair I could find was in a far distant corner of the room, so I went and sat on that. Otto Preminger looked hard at Terry and said, 'You have got a good face. You could be the furniture removal man.' And then, slightly puzzled, he looked over at me sitting in the distant corner, then back at Terry, and said, 'Do you two *have* to work together?'

Before Terry had time to reply, I retorted, 'If the furniture's very heavy, we'd prefer to.'

Everybody else in the room burst out laughing — except Otto Preminger, who scowled and ushered us out. And even though it had probably lost Terry the job, he just couldn't stop laughing. And that was the downfall of our meeting with the Hollywood tyrant.

Apart from *Hugh and I*, Terry and I used to travel the country together doing an act for the clubs and we used to share the driving in our respective cars, learning our lines together en route.

The Northern clubs soon taught us that applause, or the lack of it, isn't all that it seems to be.

One night we opened in a club in Burnley in Lancashire and seemed to be going down very well as we were getting lots of laughs. At the end there was a great deal of cheering but suddenly we found ourselves bombarded on stage by objects being hurled at us. We ducked, ran for cover and went to see the manager.

He explained, 'You've done well, lads. You got 80 beer mats on stage tonight which means they liked you. If they hadn't, they'd have thrown the bottles.'

On another occasion we played a miners' club and were warned we would be facing a tough audience. But they were wonderful. They laughed at all our jokes and seemed to be enjoying themselves hugely, but at the end only about three people applauded. Later, in the bar Terry asked one of them why. I've never forgotten his answer.

'Yes, lads, it was very funny. But no one applauds us

when we come up from the mines in the morning.'

On our travels we found some time to relax. One particular occasion was at the Club Baba in Barnsley where Terry and I decided to have a night out. Terry headed straight for the gaming room and I stayed in the lounge having a few drinks. It wasn't long before I was joined by a couple of girls and, as the night wore on, found myself offering to take them home. I went to find Terry to remind him it was his turn to drive, not telling him until later that they lived 25 miles away, and we set off — me in the back with one girl and the other in the front with Terry.

He soon got fed up with driving and turned the car off into a farmyard lane miles from anywhere. Then he produced a bottle of champagne and four glasses which we always used to carry with us — for emergencies! Just as the cork was popping, we saw the headlights of a car drawing up behind us in the lane and realised it was the police. With incredible presence of mind Terry got out of the car before they did and strolled up to them saying, 'Our names are Terry Scott and Hugh Lloyd. We're playing at Greaseborough. We've had nothing to drink and we've got two girls in the car who don't want to know. What do you want?'

The bemused police sergeant looked at him and said, 'Two signed photographs, please!'

We had another hilarious run-in with the police when we were playing summer season at Margate. In our free time, Terry and I used to enjoy playing tennis together and one day we were having a knock-up on a public court when a police car, its blue light flashing, suddenly screeched to a halt by the side of the road.

Two burly coppers got out and strode meaningfully towards us as we stood there, completely baffled. Then, as they got nearer, they looked hard at us ... and burst out laughing. It transpired that they had had a call from a woman whose home overlooked the tennis courts. At this time, two of the Great Train Robbers had escaped from prison, and the lady, looking through her net curtains saw two faces that looked familiar — and promptly called the police!

The fifth series of *Hugh and I* ended in 1966 when Vi Stevens, who played Terry's mum, sadly died. This posed something of a problem for the scriptwriters because at that time it was just not the done thing for two single men to be living alone together. How times have changed! To get over this hurdle, they decided I would win £5,000 on the Premium Bonds, a small fortune in those days, and that Terry and I would embark on a world cruise. Of course, we were very excited about this prospect until we realised that the filming was all going to be done in this country! The sand dunes of Great Yarmouth became the Sahara Desert — they even borrowed a camel from somewhere which caused much consternation among the holidaymakers — Gorlestone Docks became Tangiers and a snowy glade in Hertfordshire was Japan! However, our disappointment at not getting a luxury overseas trip was overcome when we were told we had been asked to top the bill at the Royal Household Christmas Party at Windsor Castle. This is an occasion when, unlike the Royal Command Performance, the Queen actually chooses

Above left: Ready to do battle, aged 5.

Above right: On one of our annual holidays to Llanfairfechan: myself, Mum, Dad and Nainy.

Below: Aged 15, with Form Four at the King's School. I'm third from the right, middle row.

A picture taken while I was in training for the Merchant Navy at the Wireless College, Colwyn Bay.

Read All About It! I return to the scene of my first career as a reporter for the *Chester Chronicle.*

Above: With Harvey Kirkpatrick, as our double act Doyle Devan and Scott Harvey.

Below: My *Entertainments Magazine* concert party in 1940.

Above: Entertaining the troops in Iceland with ENSA (which stood for Every Night Something Awful).

Below: An early picture of me with Terry Scott and old Chester chum, ventriloquist Jack Reid.

Above: Hard at work during a summer season in Southend. Terry Scott and I judged the bathing beauty contest.

Below left: The Gaiety Revels Show at Ventnor, Isle of Wight, my first engagement after ENSA. (Left to right) Wilfred and Joan Wallace (pianist), show producers Will Tissington and Catherine Craig, my first wife Anne Rodgers and me.

Below right: My dead-pan act, Felixstowe, 1955.

Above: The cast of *Boeing Boeing* (left to right) Me, Christina Taylor, Dandy Nichols, Ann Sidney, Jimmy Thompson and Vicki Woolf.

Below: A celebration party with some of the *Birds of Paradise* cast at Bournemouth.

Above: With the late John le Mesurier at a Concert Artistes Association dinner.

Below: With the great Tony Hancock in *Punch and Judy Man*. Tony was one of the greatest comedy actors and a unique person.

the acts she wants, so it was a particular honour for us. Also on the bill were the irrepressible Frankie Howerd and singer Kathy Kirby.

We consulted the organiser Peter Brough as to what sort of act we should do and he suggested our Two Parsons routine for which we had become quite well known.

In this act, Terry and I dressed as two clergymen in pince-nez, dog-collars and carrying prayer books. It was a load of hokum but generally went down very well with audiences.

On the great night, we knew Her Majesty was in the front row but we couldn't see her from the wings and didn't know who else was sitting by her. And when we walked on we had the shock of our lives — on one side of her was the Dean of Windsor, on the other another noted clergyman, both wearing pince-nez and both dressed exactly the same as we were! There was a moment of silence. They looked at us ... we looked at them ... and all of us, including the Queen, collapsed into laughter with tears pouring down our faces! Of course, people sitting in the rows behind had no idea what was going on and were mystified to see these two strange-looking fellows come on stage and promptly burst out laughing.

It was a good few minutes before we could pull ourselves together to start the act. It went down very well with the audience but I'm not sure the laughter was any louder at the finish than at the beginning. Afterwards, while meeting the Queen she was kind enough to say how much she had enjoyed it.

Another great thrill was to learn that Sophia Loren was a great fan of ours. She was over in Britain shooting *The Countess of Hong Kong* directed by Charlie Chaplin, and was interviewed by the newspapers who asked her how she spent her free time when she wasn't on set.

She told them that she made herself a snack and then just lay on the bed watching television. When asked what her favourite programme was, she purred, 'I just love watching *Hugh and I*!'

The thought of Sophia Loren lying on her bed watching *us* certainly had a powerful effect on myself and Terry!

After our 'world cruise' had finished, we launched on the seventh and final series of *Hugh and I* which was shown at the start of 1968. However, because Vi Stevens was no longer with us it was retitled *Hugh and I Spy*, which was a pun on the American TV series *I Spy*, then showing in the UK, and featured us returning from our globetrotting but then getting mixed up in a variety of comedy adventures, with each episode ending in a cliffhanger.

After this last series, John Chapman understably tired of writing for two idiots like us and writer Jimmy Perry, who has been responsible for creating so many TV comedy series both by himself and along with David Croft, wrote *The Gnomes of Dulwich* for us.

It was a clever idea and they were first-rate scripts, but it was limited and so we only ran to six episodes.

The programme was described as being like *The Flowerpot Men* for grown-ups! Terry and I played garden gnomes — he was called Big and I was Small — living a clandestine existence alongside our oblivious human owners.

The storylines were about the clashes between the solid British stone gnomes of 25 Telegraph Road led by us and a gnome called Old played by John Clive and our plastic European counterparts. It could almost be applicable to many situations today! There were lots of arguments about racial and cultural differences and satirical digs at the Common Market.

The series was a nightmare from an actor's point of view as we had to spend hours in make-up to get the stone effect and the costumes, which we had to sit around in all day, were hot and heavy.

The end of *The Gnomes of Dulwich* heralded the end of our television partnership. We did work together again from time to time, but it was really the right moment to go our separate ways.

Long after our partnership split up, I was told by close friends that plans had been afoot years before to do my *This Is Your Life* in the days when it was hosted by Eamonn Andrews. I discovered that they had been contacted by the programme's researchers and, of course, one obvious contact during the run of *Hugh and I* was Terry.

But I gather the whole venture had to be scrapped as Terry had told the programme makers that I had got wind of it and knew they were planning to do my *Life*.

This was absolutely untrue as I knew nothing about it until a few years ago when my friends revealed what had happened. It was just Terry's way of making sure I didn't get any of the glory, which was just typical of him.

Of course, Terry's *This Is Your Life* went ahead and I gladly appeared, but Terry had always seemed to harbour some strange resentment at my getting any recognition.

I was very sad, of course, to hear of his death in 1994. We had some wonderful times together, in spite of being such different personalities, and I have a lot of happy memories.

It's always a shame when a TV partnership has to come to an end one way or another, but in this case it was definitely time to move on.

7

It's Behind You!

Pantomime has always been a magical time for me. And wonderful as it is for an actor, it is also of great importance because it brings many children to live theatre for the first time. Hopefully, it is a love that will stay with them for the rest of their lives.

Having written my first pantomime at the age of eight, I had to wait until I was 24 before I was to appear in my first professional production. I had the cheek of the devil in those days and answered an advertisement in *The Stage* for a principal comic in *Red Riding Hood* at the Lincoln Theatre.

I applied to a man called Rex Deering who was based in Manchester and managed about five other pantomimes. He gave me the job as top of the bill without ever having met me or seen me work. I was to be paid £20 a week for three shows a day.

One day a telegram arrived to say that the actor who played the Giant in *Jack and the Beanstalk* at another venue had been taken ill. As Rex Deering wrote and produced all his own pantos he was the only one who could take over the part. The only trouble was that Rex had never walked on stilts before. So he told Jack, the principal boy, 'If I fall over, for God's sake come on and kill me quickly!'

After that first somewhat hairy season, I was hooked. In my half a century of doing pantomimes, I must have played just about every role a male performer could, from Buttons to Ugly Sister, Dame to Baron Hardup.

And I've been lucky enough to have been helped and given advice by some of the best in the business. In one of my earliest pantomimes at the New Theatre, Cardiff, I was understudying a famous Old-Time Music Hall comedian called Billy Danvers. At the end of the panto, I told him how much I'd learned from his performances. And he said, 'I came to see you in one of the understudy rehearsals and I have learned something from you. If you want to stay young in showbusiness, never stop learning.'

It's a lesson I have never forgotten, and I've loved every minute of it. But there's one part of it I absolutely hate — extraordinary though it may seem for one who has spent so many years in the theatre — and it's the dressing up. I can't stand all the changing from one costume to another and putting on make-up. I love the work but I'd far rather go on stage in my own T-shirt and trousers. People can't quite believe it when I tell them. They say, 'Well, why did you become an actor, then?' But the dressing up to me is such a minor part of it all. I've never been one of those actors who suddenly 'becomes' their character when they step into costume or has to go off and 'research their role' by spending a day in a police station or a hospital to play a copper or a doctor. After all, we're supposed to be actors, aren't we? And actors *act*, not learn to take over somebody else's job.

So pantomime became a way of life for me over the years and it is a comfort for many actors who might have had a bad year to know that at least they can earn a few bob and be in work for a few weeks over the festive season. Not to mention having a lot of fun, too, although panto is very hard work.

I teamed up with Terry Scott for panto on a few occasions. The most memorable was in 1967 at the venue of all pantomime venues, the London Palladium.

Terry and I were the Ugly Sisters starring alongside Cliff Richard and the Shadows. It was certainly a star-studded cast that included Jack Douglas and *Onedin Line* star Peter Gilmore.

I used to hold tea parties in my dressing room and most of the cast, including Cliff, would come along. Mind you, after the shows people would pop in for something a little stronger and, in fact, I gave Cliff his first ever gin and tonic, but as I believe he doesn't drink now it was probably his last. Sundays were our day off and, at the time of our run, our dressing rooms were used at night-time by various people who were appearing in televised shows.

We normally used to leave notes inviting them to help themselves to the booze we had left there. The Barron Knights used my room once and did help themselves, and left me a lovely 'thank you' note complete with a magnum of champagne.

Terry, however, was not so lucky! He returned to the Palladium one Monday to find his dressing room in a terrible state. There were sandwiches trampled into the carpet and drinks spilled everywhere.

Terry was beside himself with rage, especially when he discovered that the Rolling Stones had used his room! All sorts of arguments ensued, with the Stones claiming it was a foreign television company who were responsible for the mess.

A few days later, Terry and I were due to appear on a live TV show with Eamonn Andrews ... and the Rolling Stones! Drinks preceded the show and in the hospitality room Terry spotted Mick Jagger heading towards us. All the way to the studios he had been raging about what he was going to say about the state of his dressing room. Now was his moment of glory!

Mick walked up, shook us both by the hand and said, 'I just had to tell you that we came to see your pantomime last Wednesday and you were both wonderful. I think you're the funniest ugly sisters I've ever seen.'

Terry was speechless! It had completely taken the wind out of his sails and there was no mention of the dressing room incident after that. But he was never too successful with the Rolling Stones. On another occasion he was doing a television interview and absolutely slated the group. When he walked off, he commented to an attractive blonde standing in the shadows as to how awful he thought they were. Terry was never very good at recognising people. It was Marianne Faithfull — at the time, Mick Jagger's girlfriend.

He had a run in, too, with one of the main stars in the panto — Tanya the Baby Elephant! She was an adorable creature and would knock down every argument that animal fanatics have about training animals to appear in shows. Tanya loved every moment of it. In the wings when the music was on, she would go into her own little dance routine and I never once saw anyone having to persuade her to do anything.

However, Terry wasn't all that keen on her, as she once pushed him down a flight of stairs.

While we were appearing at the Palladium, my mum, who was now nearly 80, came to London to see the show. I took her round in the car to see the sights of the city but what fascinated her most was seeing the girls touting for trade on the roadside. She couldn't believe her eyes and kept saying, 'Drive round again ... drive round again.' Of course, you never saw anything like that in respectable Chester!

While the show was on and my mother was at home in Chester, I used to call her every Sunday night just to see how she was — my father had died some years previously.

At the time, there was a popular radio show called *Five to Ten* — known to everybody as the God Spot — in which well-known people would be asked about their religious beliefs, or lack of them. Terry and I were both asked to be on the show, and knowing my mum usually listened to it I rang her after Terry's interview to see if she had heard it, which she had.

I asked her what she had thought of it and she paused for a moment before replying, 'Well, dear, I thought he was very kind to God.'

The following year, Terry and I teamed up as the Ugly Sisters again, this time for the BBC Christmas Pantomime which was televised. But 1968 saw us back on stage again at Wimbledon Theatre, this time in *Robin Hood*. I played a robber along with actor John Gower and Terry played Martha the Nurse. Also heading the cast list was the great Dickie Henderson, at the time resident comedian-compère of *Sunday Night at the London Palladium* and star of his own series *The Dickie Henderson Show*. He played Nicholas the Sheriff's Page and Peter Gilmore was back with us again as Robin Hood.

That's the thing about the theatre, especially pantomimes. You work with someone closely for several weeks — almost living together — and then don't see them for years, and then suddenly they pop up again and it's as though it was only yesterday that you were working together! I was to find myself back at Wimbledon Theatre seven years later in what was probably the most memorable pantomime I have ever done, but it was an experience I would not wish to repeat.

I was booked to play the Dame in *Dick Whittington* with Jimmy Tarbuck. At that time of year, colds and 'flu are always prevalent, especially in the theatre where you are in such close proximity to one another and changing in and out of costumes all the time, so bugs always circulate like wildfire.

I went down with raging 'flu and had to have a couple of days off, which I hated. The doctor said I wasn't to go back to work for a week but we showbiz people are a determined bunch and I decided to disobey him and went back far too early.

I was overjoyed to be back but I was also dosed up to the eyeballs with penicillin.

In the show, I used to do a comedy trip on my entrance, in the middle of the stage. But this night, I was so delighted to be in front of an audience again that I pranced on to the stage, light-headed and full of adrenalin and somehow forgot to do my trip until I reached the footlights! I somersaulted head first into the orchestra pit! The audience roared with laughter; they thought it was all part of the act until I emerged with blood streaming from my head where I had caught the side of one of the cymbals. The curtain was temporarily rung down while the theatre manager called 999 for an ambulance, but being an astute man he had also tipped off Fleet Street so when I arrived at the Casualty Department there was a *Daily Mirror* photographer waiting for me. There I was, covered in blood, still in my Dame make-up, frock and fishnet tights and this bloke said, 'Give us a smile, Hugh.' So I did ... well, business is business! After my head had been stitched up, I told them my car was at the theatre but asked if I could possibly borrow the ambulance to rush me back there as I could just make it for the finale. They agreed and we hurtled back to Wimbledon Theatre, blue light flashing and siren wailing, and got there just as Jimmy Tarbuck was taking his bow. He saw me in the wings and called me on, and standing there on stage with my bandaged head I got the biggest round of applause I have ever had in my life! But it's certainly not something I would wish to repeat!

I was certainly very popular in that panto, but I also know how it feels to be the most *unpopular* member of the cast. In fact, one year I went from being a favourite to decidedly out-of-favour in a matter of seconds! I was playing Buttons in *Cinderella* at Newcastle Theatre Royal with Bill Simpson who used to be Doctor Finlay.

While we were rehearsing the show at the theatre, my beloved home town football team Chester City were playing Newcastle in the FA Cup and I was able to go and see the match. It was a draw, so there had to be a replay which was to be at Chester.

Obviously, I was unable to see that game as it happened to coincide with the opening night of the panto. After the first show, which was highly successful, the Lord Mayor held a civic reception for us at the theatre. While he was making a very warm complimentary speech about us, someone approached him and whispered something in his ear.

He stopped mid-speech and said, 'Ladies and gentlemen, it's not all good news tonight. I have just heard that Newcastle has lost to Chester in the third round of the FA Cup.'

A solitary cheer went up in the auditorium. I just couldn't help myself and everybody turned to look at me with horrified expressions.

After all that glowing praise, I suddenly became the most hated person in the room.

My roles in panto, of course, chopped and changed. In fact, I didn't play Buttons for much longer as by this time I was becoming more of a 'buttons popping off' character with my slightly expanded girth. So I was probably a little better off covered up in a voluminous Ugly Sister costume when I teamed up with Scots actor Russell Hunter who became famous for playing the smelly character Lonely in the hit TV series *Callan*. That highly skilled comedian, dancer and acrobat Billy Dainty was playing Buttons, and Michael Aspel's estranged wife Lizzie Power took the role of Prince Charming.

But it was our Ugly Sister stage names I will never forget — I was Hunkamunka and Russell was Dollalolla!

One of the most star-studded pantos I have appeared in was at Richmond Theatre in Surrey in 1983, which conveniently was only a ten-minute drive from my home, then in nearby East Sheen.

It was *Dick Whittington* and starred Roy Hudd as Idle Jack, June Whitfield as Fairy Bowbells, Honor Blackman as Queen Rat and Dickie 'Stinker' Murdoch as Alderman Fitzwarren. I was playing the Mate to the Captain, played by Allen Christie, and the role of Sarah the Cook was played by famous panto dame Jack Tripp. As well as that, TV presenter Sarah Greene was Alice, Arthur Askey's daughter Anthea was a marvellous Tommy the Cat and *Desert Song* star John Hanson played the Sultan of Morocco. Dick Whittington was played by a bubbly redhead Geraldine Gardner who had legs so long they didn't know when to quit. Sadly, she died tragically a few years ago.

I shared a dressing room with Dickie Murdoch and John Hanson — what a trio! Dickie always used to insist on a particular brand of face cream as it was just right for his skin. He used pots of it and was frequently sending people out in the middle of a show to get him some more. John Hanson always wore a black wig off stage. He was quite open about it as he explained that he still got tons of fan mail from adoring females who had seen him in the *Desert Song* and he thought they would like to remember him as he was, not with grey hair as it would make them feel their age, too! As for me, well I spent most of my time up and down the stone stairs backstage taking showers!

Roy and I did a hilarious slapstick kitchen scene together which involved us hurling the most revolting gunk at each other and getting covered in it, then having to rush backstage to shower before the next scene.

The dressing-room and shower conditions were a bit primitive as it was a few years before Richmond Theatre underwent a dramatic backstage refurbishment, creating a luxurious and individual style all of its own.

As I didn't live far from the theatre, some of the cast members used to come back to my place between the matinée and the evening show. Roy and his girlfriend Debbie, who is now his wife, would come over and he would have a cup of tea or a bottle of pale ale while we had a game on my billiard table. Geraldine's tastes were a little more sophisticated. She had a penchant for champagne and anchovy sandwiches! As I said, she was a tall girl with extraordinarily long legs and a mane of red curly hair. One day, on the way to a matinée she found herself stuck in a horrendous traffic jam in the West End. Realising she was never going to get there on time unless she did something drastic, she leapt out of the car, hailed a passing police car and told them, 'I'm Dick Whittington ... help me!' And they did! While one took care of her car, the other rushed her, siren wailing, to Richmond Theatre and got her there in the nick of time. All of us men in the panto reckoned we wouldn't have got the same treatment if we'd tried it.

Mind you, I was helped out of the same kind of sticky spot when I was appearing at the Beck Theatre in Hayes, Middlesex, in *Cinderella* with Frank Carson and Wendy Richard. On the way to the theatre my car broke down, right outside a florist's shop. Panicking, I dashed into the shop and asked if I could use the phone to ring a taxi. The very sweet girl in there, hearing my tale of woe, offered to drive me in her florist's van to the theatre, which she did. I thought of sending her flowers as a thank you but realised that would be a bit like sending coals to Newcastle. So I sent her some tickets for the show instead, and she came backstage so everybody could meet my guardian angel.

Frank Carson, who was playing Buttons, was a great guy. But working with him was like doing a completely different show every night. Although to the audience it looks like total chaos, on stage it is, in fact, very organised, disciplined chaos which has been well rehearsed. It has to be.

But not in Frank's book! Often, he could be found up in the bar laughing and cracking jokes with the front-of-house staff and people who had just popped in for a drink five or ten minutes before he was due on stage. He was so laid back, unlike the rest of us, that you had to laugh, but he certainly got my adrenalin going every night that season!

As Baron Hardup, I did a comedy gag routine with Frank in which I was his feed. I came on first, supposedly followed by Frank, but I never knew which side he would appear from, or when, or if he would already be on stage! And when it came to the jokes, I never knew which order he was going to do it in that night or what he was going to say. It was hysterical! I did have great admiration for Frank in the way that he dealt with the handicapped children we had in the audience. He teased them and was jokingly rude to them, just as he was with able-bodied children, and they loved him for it, because he didn't make them feel that they were different.

In the mid-Eighties, I moved from my London home to the Sussex coast and in my first year there wanted my agent to get me panto at Brighton which was close to my home in the village of Rottingdean.

I was booked to guest star as Baron Hardup in *Cinderella* at the Theatre Royal and there began a long and lasting friendship with the pantomime producer John Nathan-Turner who was also at the time the highly-respected producer of *Doctor Who*. It was probably the best and most original panto I have ever done.

Buttons was played by the lovely Colin Baker, who was also Doctor Who at the time, Dandini was Wendy Richard — we seemed to have been following each other around since my *Hugh and I* days — and Mirazel the Fairy Godmother was played by Carol Kaye of the Kaye Sisters.

The Ugly Sisters were James Court and David Raven, a great character who still calls me Daddy as he was playing my daughter, and well known on the West End drag queen scene as Maisie Trollette. The panto was choreographed by Gary Downie, a former West End dancer who had by now gone into television.

John devised the most hysterical scene which was kept a closely guarded secret and, even on the Press Night, the reviewers agreed not to describe it so as not to spoil the surprise for future audiences. He teamed Colin, Carol and myself up to form the Chaos Sisters, who were to be the cabaret at the Prince's ball. Colin and I wore identical Kaye Sisters wigs to match Carol's hair, and we all wore strapless, luminous pink, sequinned dresses. Colin was about a foot taller than me so they put me in the middle as the one who always got everything wrong in our 'Chattanooga Choo Choo' routine. It brought the house down!

A few years later, I played Dame again — dreading the thought of all those costume changes — in *Babes in the Wood* at the Churchill Theatre in Bromley, Kent, with Welsh singer Max Boyce as Robin Hood. The Churchill is a lovely venue but whoever designed it certainly hadn't got the actors in mind as the dressing rooms are right down in the bowels of the earth and you don't see the outside world from the moment you arrive for a matinée at lunchtime until leaving in the pitch black at night. We used to say we felt like Santa's gnomes beavering away with no idea what went on outside. Added to that, we had to walk up numerous stairs in heavy costumes to get to the stage as it was obvioulsy forbidden to use the lift during performances in case we got stuck in it. But we did have a lot of fun that season along with Sheila Steafel playing Fairy Godmother and Arthur Bostrom, best known as the 'Good Moaning' policeman in *'Allo 'Allo* as Little John.

One of the young boy dancers in the chorus was gay and he confided to us that he had a problem as his mother was coming to see the show and she didn't know. He had moved his boyfriend out temporarily so that she could stay and had deliberately untidied his flat so she didn't get suspicious.

In one of his roles as one of the Merry Men, he was passed a message from the wings which read something like, 'Robin has escaped and is on his way.' However, on the night his mother was in the audience, one of the mischievous backstage staff had rewritten the message to read, 'Robin has escaped and thinks it's about time that you told your mother you were gay.' The poor lad started to read it ... and then nearly collapsed in hysterics on stage.

I've had offers for panto since the last one I did at the De La Warr Pavilion in Bexhill in 1997, but really I'm not interested any more.

That season in Bexhill was enough to put me off panto for life, with very poor backstage facilities — three of us had to share a small, dingy, freezing cold room with a stone floor, and it had a walk-out from the stage that felt as though it was going to collapse every time I made my entrance.

So few places put on proper, traditional pantos these days, which, I don't care what anybody says, the children still adore. They just put a body into a costume to walk around as a Power Ranger or an Action Man, or they employ retired sports stars or Australian soap stars at great expense, half of whom don't even know what a pantomime is. People who would have paid to see Stanley Matthews play football would not have wanted to pay to see him play cricket. I think that people in the public eye sometimes get exalted opinions of themselves and believe that people want to see them do anything. And there are always those stupid and greedy enough to allow them to do it.

I'm all for change and keeping up with the times, but pantomime has a wonderful tradition that is unique to us in Britain and it would be such a shame if that joy was lost for future generations to come.

8

Hamburgers and Crumpets – My Life Down Under

My first trip down under was something of a 'honeymoon' cruise. The summer after Josie and I had split up, I decided to take a holiday on my own to Jersey where I spent a lonely, miserable week. But returning to the mainland, I met a girl called Carole Wilkinson and there was an instant mutual attraction.

Carole and I were inseparable from the moment we met and she came with me to Newquay in Cornwall where I was running an Old-Time Music Hall.

When Carole moved into my flat in Maida Vale, it helped Josie — by mutual agreement — to get a divorce on the grounds of my adultery, and Carole and I were married shortly afterwards in 1969. Unlike my other wives, Carole had no career ambitions. She'd tried being an art teacher but that didn't last very long, and consequently she became bored being on her own while I was working. Inevitably, I suppose, the boredom led to her having affairs and after a while we split up.

But, as with my other wives, we stayed friendly and then we had a mutually agreed divorce in the mid-Seventies.

Carole and I had married just two months before I was due to go to Australia for a year touring in a Ray Cooney and John Chapman farce called *Not Now, Darling.*

I had been offered first-class plane tickets to fly out there but I'm never keen on flying unless I absolutely have to and managed to swap them for a sea voyage. And so Carole and I found ourselves back at sea again, on a somewhat bigger vessel than the one on which we had met, for this time we were to make the trip on the *Canberra.*

The journey took four weeks and in that time we made lots of friends, including a couple called Alan and Kathy Martin who were disembarking at Melbourne where they lived, while we were getting off further on in Sydney where the play was being rehearsed.

Alan told me he was a milkman, but when they got off at Melbourne we noticed they got into a gleaming, chauffeur-driven Rolls-Royce that was waiting for them by the quayside. I decided I must be in the wrong job if that was the kind of money Australian milkmen earned, but then I discovered that Alan owned one of the biggest dairies in Melbourne, and he was, in fact, Matt Munro's father-in-law! We were to spend many happy times socialising with them, and Matt and his wife, when we arrived in Melbourne a few weeks later.

Within 24 hours of docking at Sydney, I discovered we had landed, unintentionally, right in the middle of the seamy — or should I say steamy — side of life! We had rented a flat in King's Cross — like its counterpart in London, a pretty dubious area of the city. Carole set off with a list of things to buy at the local newsagent's, including, on the advice of my accountant, an address book and a cash book. The friendly newsagent chatted away happily until she reached those two items and his attitude changed.

With a knowing wink and a leer he said, 'Setting up in business are you, darling?' That was our introduction to Australia.

The play's director, Patrick Cargill, had a pretty memorable one, too. He had just stepped off the boat and was immediately whisked off to a press conference. Not having had a chance to see anything or meet anyone properly, one of the first questions fired at him was, 'How do you find Australians?'

Feeling considerably tired and a bit disgruntled, he gave a classic answer, 'Every bloody where!'

After rehearsing, we travelled to Newcastle in New South Wales where we opened at the Hunter Theatre and ran with tremendous success for two weeks.

However, our next stop was Melbourne and on arrival there we found that the theatre had been 'dark' — closed down — for the past three months. Consequently, the taxi driver I had hired to take me there, and who hadn't been in

Melbourne long, had never heard of it and hadn't an earthly clue where it was. Its closure was also somewhat reflected in some of the audiences we had at the beginning of our three-month run there.

The so-called 'society' of the city tended to be far more snobbish than anywhere else in Australia. For instance, those who had got front row seats tended to arrive just after the curtain went up to make sure they were noticed. It didn't help us on stage at all.

I played the part of Arnold Crouch, a mild-mannered fur salon owner, and Ron Frazer, a very well-known Australian actor played Gilbert Bodley, co-owner of Bodley, Bodley and Crouch. He played the part of a lecher — a charming, elegant man whom women swooned over.

In real life, he was totally charming to everybody ... and he was gay.

Ron and I had become great mates by now. One day, we were in a taxi and, seeing a pretty girl walk by, I said, 'There's a nice bit of crumpet!' Ron replied that it was all very well for me, but he hadn't got a name for men he fancied. From then on, he decided he would call them 'hamburgers'.

When I was back home one Christmas, he sent me a card saying he had spent a quiet day with his mother but on Boxing Day God obviously thought he had been good as he sent him 'a hamburger big enough to feed the whole of Biafra!'

Some time later, Australian television did Ron's *This Is Your Life*. They had offered to fly me over to appear on it but I was committed to a stage play at the time and couldn't go, so I did a taped interview, where, after giving the usual glowing tributes, I said, 'Ron and I were great friends. We never disagreed about anything much — except we had different tastes in food. I like crumpets and he likes hamburgers.'

Of course, Ron just fell about laughing in the studio much to the astonishment of all the other guests who had absolutely no clue what the joke was all about.

While in Melbourne, Carole made quite a name for herself. As the wife of a visiting celebrity, she was asked to go along and give a talk to a Melbourne Ladies' Society about wine-tasting. For some unknown reason, they seemed to assume she was an expert on the subject.

Carole was quite an outrageous lady, and not, I think, what they were expecting. After a lavish lunch they sat eagerly awaiting her speech.

She stood up and said, 'Well, as long as it's wet and alcoholic — I'll drink it!' And promptly sat down again.

From Melbourne we went to Brisbane where we were met by a thunderstorm and the most horrific flat I have ever spent the night in. All the furniture was plastic and there was no air-conditioning.

What with that and the raging thunderstorm, we moved out to a hotel the very next day. In Canberra, our next stop, the show attracted a lot of members of the Australian Government and we, in turn, were invited to be an audience at a sitting of their Parliament. One memorable moment was hearing the former Prime Minister John Gorton giving an impressive performance on one issue to the point where he almost boiled over, banging the table with rage. It was only at the end of his oration that I realised his temper was all over a dispute about the Parliamentary catering system!

We returned to Newcastle before finishing the tour in Sydney where unfortunately there was no theatre available for us at the time. We ended up in a theatre restaurant in the suburbs which was not a good idea judging by the audiences.

Incidentally, it was at that time I was to meet Peggy Mount, who was appearing in a Sydney Theatre, for the first time. Of course, I went on to work with her many times both in television and on stage.

It was in a restaurant in Sydney that I was almost elevated to royal status! One night, dining out, my appearance created some excitement for two middle-aged ladies sitting at a nearby table. Eventually, they came over and one asked if she could shake me by the hand as she had been to see the show the previous night. I happily obliged and she informed me that the Queen had been in the city the week before for the centenary of Sydney Harbour and that she had shaken hands with Her Majesty herself. Then, in a booming voice, she turned and announced to the entire restaurant, 'Just think — last week, the Queen — this week, Hugh Lloyd!'

Our first Christmas Day in Australia was spent in Sydney with friends of Carole's father — like him, ex-airforce people — at their home in Cottage Point on the outskirts of the city. They had a lovely house right on the top of a cliff where you had to leave your car and make your way down a rickety path to get there. But they had a lovely view over the river that flowed out from Sydney Harbour, and had a small open launch moored below.

But lovely though it was, the whole day turned out to be a bit of a disaster for me. It seemed very strange to be sitting in the sweltering heat of around 100°F eating roast turkey and all the trimmings, and after lunch I fell asleep under an umbrella. However, I was wearing shorts and didn't realise my knees had been poking out into the sunshine and when I woke up they were a mass of blisters. That was bad enough, but what made it worse was that one of the vital parts of the play involved me crawling around on my hands and knees. For the next few weeks, I played the role in complete agony.

When the play was finished, I was sad to leave Australia but at the same time happy to be going home. I'd also signed a television contract to return to Oz in nine months' time, so I knew it wasn't farewell for ever. I managed to get us a free trip back on a ship called the *Northern Star* in return for doing two Sunday concerts for them on board. Our homeward route took us via Wellington, Auckland, the West Indies, Curaçao, Barbados and Acapulco. The Captain and his crew were a great bunch and I wrote them a song, a parody on Lee Marvin's hit song from the film *Paint Your Wagon*, 'Wandering Star'. It went:

I was born on the Northern Star
I was born near the Cocktail Bar
Mother was a passenger
Father was one of the crew
It might have been a steward but
I don't know exactly who …

And so on. This became a favourite with crew members and passengers and often when trips ashore were made you could hear the strains of my song across the dark waters as the merry passengers returned to the boat in small launches.

On these shore expeditions, some of the crew members often returned well the worse for drink and in fighting mood. The Chief Petty Officer, however, had his own method of dealing with them. He stood barely 4ft high — but he was 4ft in all directions — and packed as good a punch as any professional boxer. If any of his returning shipmates looked like causing trouble, he would promptly knock them out cold before they had a chance to say a word and would have them carried to their cabins. I'm pleased to say he didn't practise the same technique on the passengers!

The Captain was a man who enjoyed a drink and he held so many cocktail parties that he used to have a cold shower fully dressed after one session to sober up for the next.

When I returned to Australia nine months later as arranged, it was to do a TV series, a joint venture with the BBC and Australian television, called *Birds in the Bush*. The money for it was put up by a Hungarian, George Rockhey, who had emigrated to Australia.

The same version of the programme was televised in the UK under the title *The Virgin Fellas*. In Australia it was a smash hit ... over here it was a terrible flop! Again, I was to star with my old chum Ron Frazer and the lovely Ann Sydney and the series was directed by David Croft.

I played an Englishman who had inherited a farm in the outback and my distant Australian cousin (Ron Frazer) had come to help me with it. But part of my legacy was also to inherit a bevy of young, leggy orphan girls whom my late uncle had supposedly adopted.

It was in this series that I was to have my first proper attempt at riding a horse. I had insisted on a quiet creature that was not likely to shoot off like a bolt out of the blue. My wish was granted — but to the extreme. The horse they gave me was so quiet it almost refused to budge and when it did eventually move, it literally picked its way from blade of grass to blade of grass! When filming started, the girls, who were riding bareback, had disappeared into the distance leaving me hanging on to the neck of my mount which had only just started plodding very slowly across the set.

You may think from this that horses and I don't mix, but I should point out that I am moderately interested in horse-racing. On Saturdays, I have my 50p each way on horses I can watch on the TV because it makes the racing more interesting. But I actually once owned one-twelfth of a race-horse called Dairywood, a co-ownership which was instigated by the lovely Felix Bowness who played the jockey in the hit TV series *Hi-de-Hi* and who, in real life, is racing mad. On one occasion, Felix took me to Fontwell Races where his old friend Josh Gifford — the champion jockey at the time and now a great trainer — was riding. We went round to see Josh and asked him for some tips.

'Well,' he said, 'I've got two horses here this afternoon and three horses here tomorrow and I can't tell you what will win. But I can tell you that I shall win the Two O'Clock at Newbury next Saturday.'

And he did. On a horse that came in at 100–8. When I saw Josh again some time later, he said that, occasionally, my horse would be in a race in which it should beat all the others — barring accidents, of course. Well, my horse, Dairywood, came nowhere in its first two races because the trainer said it didn't like other horses. The third race it won at 20–1 and the fourth race it also won at about 8–1. By this time, the whole of Newquay, where I was running an Old-Time Music Hall, knew about my wonderful horse and backed it in its fifth race. Needless to say, it came nowhere ... and, in fact, that's the last we ever saw of it, so my racing entrepreneur days ended abruptly. Today I'm just an armchair gambler.

* * *

It's always said there are plenty of sharks in showbusiness but I've never come nearer to them than the day I sank in Sydney Harbour. We were filming a scene on a liner which was supposed to be sinking, and I played the part of a man disregarding the 'women and children first' order and jumped into a dinghy. What was not in the script was that the dinghy actually started to sink, and I found myself gradually disappearing into shark-infested Sydney Harbour with the entire film crew falling about laughing. Needless to say, they eventually hauled me out but it took quite a time to see the funny side of it, especially as I hate actually being in the water and don't swim! Shortly after that, I got infective hepatitis. The doctors said it was from drinking from a contaminated cup in the studio canteen. It rather held up the series as I had to be isolated in my hotel room for four weeks and the entire cast had to be inoculated. But it didn't put me off going back to Australia and a few years later, in 1976, I returned having been asked to make a guest appearance in Sir Arthur Pinero's *The Magistrate* at the Festival of Perth.

When I arrived, I was also asked to read the lesson in a church service. I duly dressed up in my Sunday best, but my suit and tie were not the best choice for the 100°F temperatures! There were 1,000 people in the congregation but the only ones dressed up were myself and the Governor General. Everybody else was in short-sleeved shirts and shorts.

The climate was about the same for our opening night in the play, but in the theatre, the air-conditioning had broken down. By the third act, the originally enthusiastic audience had become a blur of waving programmes which they were using as fans to keep themselves cool.

I made the closing speech but that night added my own version which would have made Sir Arthur turn in his grave! The correct closing words were, 'This is my heir in whom I am well pleased and I am going to change his ways.' But I altered it to, 'Little did Sir Arthur know when he wrote this play back in 1891 that his last line would be most appropriate here and now when he said what was needed was heir-conditioning.'

I will never forget life Down Under. My reviews in the papers there were pretty varied. I was called a 'doll', referred to as not even remotely resembling a Che Guevara of Britain (whatever that meant), and one paper said I was probably the only man in the world who could manage to look quite sexless with my hands under the fur coat of a naked actress! Perhaps, though, my favourite quote comes from my co-star Ron Frazer, who sadly died suddenly a few years ago. He told one newspaper that with a lace doily on my head and a candle in my hand I was the spitting image of Queen Victoria!

9

Butlers, Corpses and Ear Trumpets

When I tell my more 'legitimate' colleagues in the theatre that I once took over from Dame Sybil Thorndyke, it's a bit of a conversation stopper, to put it mildly. But it happens to be true. And it's got nothing to do with dressing up in skirts. This unlikely situation transpired when, sadly, the great lady died back in 1976. Up until then she had been Chairman of our amateur Chester Theatre Club because of her husband Lewis Casson's links with the city. And I was asked to take her place, a position I am proud to hold to this day. I've seen so many excellent performances there and always feel I am amongst fellow professionals!

It was at Chester Theatre Club, as a boy of 14, that I was to make my first stage appearance in 'proper' theatre in a play called *The Housemaster* by Ian Hay. The lead was taken by our family GP, Dr William Scott, and I played one of his pupils.

My next appearance on stage was around three years later at Chester's Royalty Theatre in George Bernard Shaw's *You Never Can Tell.* I had a walk-on part as a waiter. But it was in this production that I learned a great lesson of the theatre — one I have never forgotten and always try to follow.

The play was produced by Dr Stefan Hock who was a colleague of the famous international director Max Reinhart. In the company was an actor called Billy Thatcher who was always fidgeting on stage.

One day, in the middle of a rehearsal, Dr Hock stopped the action and in strident tones told Billy, 'Boy, if you've got something good to say, stand still and say it!'

I was absolutely skint when I had my first taste of the West End. I had had three auditions for the famous Windmill Theatre and failed to get in. But I was given a last chance and decided that wearing a bow-tie while doing my act might clinch it. However, at the time I was living in Primrose Hill, a few miles from the heart of London, and I couldn't afford the bus fare and a bow-tie. I bought the bow-tie, walked to the West End, and on my fourth attempt got in! The Windmill was an unforgettable experience for any artiste, and was the starting ground for many famous names like Peter Sellers, Harry Secombe and Tony Hancock.

I was booked to do 30 shows a week for the princely sum of £40, which was a fortune in the Fifties. The shows started at around noon and ran continuously every hour, with just a ten-minute break in between, up until 11.00pm.

The audience consisted mainly of men who came in just to see the dancing girls in their see-through tops. Many of them would stay all day, watching the same show over and over again and while us comedians were on they would eat their pre-packed lunches of sandwiches, drink from their coffee flasks and read the newspapers! In fact, it was said that the comedians were only employed in the hope that they would drive the audiences out!

There is a marvellous story of a ballerina who made her début at the Windmill, which really sums up what it was all about. She was a classic ballerina, in the true sense of the word, and the top half of her costume was almost see-through. After she had gone through her routine, she went off-stage and, horrified, spoke to one of the comedians waiting in the wings.

'While I was dancing, there was a man in the front row playing with himself,' she told him.

The comic replied, 'My dear, in this theatre, that's applause.'

My routine was a dead-pan act and I have to say that a lot of the time the audience were looking at me with exactly the same expression on *their* faces! I lasted three seasons — and then I was sacked.

The proprietor, Vivian Van Damm had seen me on television in *Great Scott — It's Maynard*, and thought it was very funny. He wanted me to do the same routine at the Windmill. Of course, neither of us had the experience at the time to realise that what works on television doesn't always work on stage. And it didn't. I really died a death that week and very apologetically he said he would have to get rid of me. I didn't mind really. After all those silent audiences I had suffered, I was glad to go!

It wasn't until the mid-Sixties that I went back into the theatre again and one of my first appearances was in a wonderful two-hander, *Rattle of a Simple Man* — a play I have done four times with different leading ladies, including Ann Sydney, Liz Frazer and Anne Carroll. The play, as I have said, is about a Northern football fan who is a virgin in his 40s and is dared by his pals on a visit to London to sample the services of a prostitute.

I first played it in Chester where I had volunteered my services to help boost a new theatre project there. Playing opposite me was an 18-year old actress, Bridget Bryce, who went on to appear in *Coronation Street*.

A classic tale is told by another actress who also played in *Rattle*. She was sharing digs with two strippers who invited her along to the club where they were appearing to see their act. After she had been to see them perform, she thought she would return the invitation and asked them to come along and watch her.

At the end of the play, her role involves her getting very distressed and removing her make-up before getting into bed. The two strippers went backstage afterwards, full of admiration for her performance, but said in awe, 'Aren't you daring? Taking your make-up off in front of all those people!'

It was around this time that I also appeared in King and Cary's *Big Bad Mouse*. The director of that particular production was Alex Dore and I was playing Mr Bloome, while my good mate Bunny May took the part of Harold Hopkins. Alex and I both fancied one of the female members of the cast, and one day Bunny, Alex and I were walking along, while Alex and I discussed the obvious charms of the lady in question. Bunny had listened silently as the two of us carried on and then he spoke.

'I know you're the director and you are the star but I thought you two gentlemen would like to know that I'm sharing the same digs as her next week!'

I don't keep a lot of theatre memorabilia or accolades but one of my most prized possessions is a letter of congratulations and thanks from the great JB Priestley after I appeared in *When We Are Married*. I was playing Herbert Soppitt and the cast of 14 included Peggy Mount, Frank Thornton, Renee Asherson, Freda Jackson ... and the irrepressible Fred Emney.

We were rehearsing and opening the play at the Yvonne Arnaud Theatre in Guildford before our West End opening at the Strand. The afternoon of the dress rehearsal was an incredibly hot, sultry September day and we were all togged up, sweating, in our period costumes. Our only audience was the director Laurie Lister and the great Mr Priestley himself who had asked if he might sit in.

We laboured through the whole thing, with no laughs or applause, of course, getting hotter and hotter. At the end, Laurie told us to take a ten-minute break and then Priestley would read us his 'notes'.

We all stood around on stage moaning and groaning at how awful we all were and how unfunny we had been, with that dreadful insecurity that all actors have over their performances. All, that is, except Fred Emney.

Fred's huge bulk was sprawled across a sofa that was part of the scenery. He just lay there taking all this in.

As the break drew to a close and we saw Laurie and JB Priestley coming down towards the footlights, Fred, in a booming voice that filled the theatre, announced, 'Well, if he doesn't like it he shouldn't have wrote it!' Priestley just fell about laughing — he loved things like that.

In the West End, we opened to a rapturous reception. Priestley was watching the play from a box in the theatre and, at the end of the show, the audience shouted, 'Author! Author!'

He duly stood up and said, 'Ladies and gentlemen, I wrote this play 40 years ago.' Then he pointed to us, all assembled on stage. 'Tonight, the credit is theirs.'

I don't think there was a dry eye on stage at that moment.

My favourite role was in a production I did some ten years later in 1981 of Noel Coward's *Tonight at 8.30* at the West End's Lyric Theatre. It was a trilogy — *Shadow Play*, *Hands Across the Sea* (in which the lovely Susie Blake played my wife) and *Red Peppers*. The latter was a real indulgence for me as in my role as Bert Bentley I made a most unusual — and I would think unique — entrance. The action takes place mainly on the stage of the Palace of Varieties in a small English provincial town and our director Jonathan Lynn decided I should make my first appearance conducting from the orchestra pit!

Playing butlers has also seemed to be one of my fortes in life. Perhaps it's my subservient demeanour that makes them think of me for these roles. The first time I was directed by Sheila Hancock was in Pinero's *Dandy Dick* in which I played Blore the butler in a cast that included Andrew Sachs and the flamboyant Royce Ryton, who each day carried a large feather of a different colour to suit his mood! I was later to star in Royce's brilliant comedy *The Unvarnished Truth* in which my co-star was ex *Z-Cars* actor Douglas Fielding. The play involved four dead ladies, one of whom we had to keep carrying on and off stage.

Dougie and I soon discovered that we had a mutual passion — football. Both of us were great fans of different teams and were eager to hear the weekend scores as soon as they were announced. However, this presented problems as on tour we were doing Saturday matinées. We soon resolved this by arranging with the 'corpse' to find out the scores while we were on stage and, as we carried her supposedly lifeless body back on, she would whisper the respective results out of the side of her mouth.

And there is another butler role I will never forget, but for reasons no one could ever dream of. I was playing Hook in the Ben Travers farce *Thark*, along with Griff Rhys-Jones as Ronald Gamble, Dinsdale Landon as Sir Hector Benbow and *2.4 Children* star Belinda Lang as Kitty Stratton. We opened to packed houses at the Lyric, Hammersmith. Griff was a great guy to work with but a tremendous disciplinarian ... with himself. If he felt he had done something wrong on stage or hadn't been good enough, he would shut himself in the dressing room and hurl chairs about, but he was never angry with anybody else.

It was at this time, in the late Eighties, that there was the great storm that followed the earlier hurricane. Anybody who lived outside London, as I did, found it impossible to get anywhere. Trees were down, roads were blocked — the nation was in chaos! In the morning, phone calls were going backwards and forwards between pros in the Brighton area who had to get to town for various shows but it seemed it was going to be absolutely hopeless. We rang several cab firms but no one was venturing out of Sussex. It was a particular problem for me as we had no understudies so it would mean that that night's show would have to be cancelled if I couldn't get there. I felt terribly guilty but what could I do about it? Suddenly, in the middle of the afternoon, the doorbell rang. Much to my astonishment, there stood a taxi driver from one of the countless local firms that had been called, asking where I wanted to go. When I said London I expected him to react with horror but he didn't bat an eyelid!

'All right, if I stop for petrol,' he said, 'only I'm a bit low.' I made a few quick calls and we arranged to pick up a couple of dancers and a musician en route. How we eventually made it I will never know. It took hours — but we got there and I arrived at the stage door with about 15 minutes to spare, much to the astonishment of the rest of the cast. They welcomed me with open arms but, quite honestly, I'm sure they were most disappointed to see me. They were all looking forward to a rare weekday night off, and I spoilt it. It was also during that run that I can say in all honesty that I upstaged HRH Princess Margaret.

I was sharing a dressing room with a marvellous character, Peter Carlisle, who was playing another butler called Death! Peter, who was a fair age, used to walk with a long silver-tipped cane, the top of which he kept filled with his favourite tipple. He lived with his wife in Blackheath and used to make his own way home on public transport, until one night when he was mugged. He wasn't badly hurt but his naturally worried daughter insisted he must be picked up from the theatre and driven home. This presented no problem as her husband Steve worked for a very up-market limousine service in the West End so it was arranged that he would collect his father-in-law every night and drive him home before starting his later jobs from the smart clubs and restaurants. When Steve heard that I used to get a taxi or the tube to catch my train to Victoria, he offered to drop me at the station on the way.

One night, we heard that Princess Margaret was in the audience on a private visit. She was a friend of the set designer Carl Toms and had come as his guest. Afterwards, she came backstage and met us all and was most gracious.

I was eager to get off as usual to catch my train and Steve, in his normal chauffeur's uniform, was duly waiting by his Mercedes limousine. A small crowd, hearing that the Princess was there, had gathered at the stage door. They were rewarded by seeing her when she emerged to get into a small Volvo ... to be immediately followed by myself and Peter, who swept regally into our waiting limousine! Steve, who had appraised the situation, played up to it by standing to attention at the kerbside, the door open and waiting for us. The crowd just stood there open-mouthed!

We had wonderful reviews for *Thark* but I wasn't quite sure about some of the remarks about me. They left me wondering if I was a man or a menagerie. I was described as 'haunting the play with quivering chins and walrus eyes'. Michael Billington in the *Guardian* likened me to a 'lugubrious goldfish', another said I had the expression of 'a haddock on a slab' and the *Daily Mail*'s Jack Tinker called me 'an under-cooked tortoise'!

By now, it had been decided to take the play to the Savoy Theatre for a short run, as Griff was otherwise committed to his television series after that.

Thousands of pounds were taken in advance bookings and we finished on the Saturday night with a week's break to look forward to before opening in the West End. Griff is a workaholic and had been dragged off, protesting, by his long-suffering wife Jo, for a few days' break in Antigua.

On the Monday morning, the phone rang early at home. It was Peter Carlisle.

'Have you heard the news?' he said. 'The Savoy Theatre's burnt down!'

I thought he must be joking but, sadly, it was nowhere near April Fools' Day. And, of course, the lovely old theatre in the heart of London *had* burnt down.

Griff's agent sent him a wire in Antigua. It read, 'Since you've been away, apartheid has come to an end, the Berlin Wall is down ... and, by the way, the Savoy Theatre has burnt down.'

We were all heartbroken. There were efforts made to find another suitable venue but, for a short run, it proved impossible. And, sadly, *Thark* never saw the light of day again with our company. Of all the things you'd think can go wrong with a show, the theatre burning down in the centre of London is not one of them!

On the subject of the West End, I also spent two years at the Strand Theatre dropping my trousers when I played Mr Needham in *No Sex Please — We're British*. People used to ask me, 'Don't you get tired of playing the same part night after night?' And I'd always tell them, 'No, because the audience is always different.'

The show attracted a lot of foreign tourists, especially the Japanese. Usually, during the first half there would hardly be a smile from them but after the interval they would be doubled up in their seats. We had the theory that during the break an interpreter would explain the plot to them!

Some time after I had left the show, they asked me if I would go back for a few weeks to fill in for someone, which I did. But I had to learn the whole thing again because, although I have a photographic memory and can learn very quickly, as soon as a play is over I just wipe the slate clean, like a blackboard, and can't remember a word of it.

Having this kind of memory was an advantage when I joined the National Theatre company in the early Eighties. I am not usually associated with serious theatre but I actually spent a year with a prestigious company set up by Sir Ian McKellen and Edward Petherbridge. They were putting on three productions — Webster's *The Duchess of Malfi*,

Chekhov's *The Cherry Orchard* and a double bill of Sheridan's *The Critic* and Tom Stoppard's *The Real Inspector Hound*. I think I had basically been brought in as a bit of light comedy relief among all those 'real' actors by Sheila Hancock who was directing *The Critic*. I was relieved to see that also in the company was my mate Roy Kinnear — now sadly missed.

Throughout those 12 months, we kept each other sane from time to time. I can't in all honesty say the National is my favourite venue. The actors are badly paid — the management seem to think the dubious privilege of appearing there is reward enough — while the multitude of admin workers sitting around in offices undoubtedly come off best. The actors, and even the audience paying highly-inflated ticket prices, come second to them.

However, there were some enjoyable moments and we had a week in Aberdeen, a week in Paris and a month in Chicago.

Being a member of a company, I had to take part in three of the plays — all in the rep cycle at the same time — which is where my memory came in handy. I thoroughly enjoyed the farcical pageantry of *The Critic* and adored playing the old retainer Firs in *The Cherry Orchard* ... but *The Duchess of Malfi* was hardly my cup of tea ... nor Roy's! Dressed up as courtiers with about six lines between us, we relied on each other to keep awake on stage while the stars of the production were continually making long speeches, falling down dead, then getting up and making more speeches. We were glad when that one came to an end! As devotees of Chekhov will know, Firs is a wonderful part to play, especially at the end when all the family has departed and he is left on the stage to die alone as the cherry petals fall down. Highly emotive.

Quite how quickly Firs met his demise depended on whether or not the curtain had gone up in time and if I was in any danger of missing my train. If we had rung up on time or if it was a matinée and I wasn't going home between the shows, I would really milk that death scene. It was a different kettle of fish, of course, if we were running late and the stage hands would always say, 'Ten minutes late tonight. Firs is going to die quickly!'

As I said, we spent a week in Aberdeen at His Majesty's Theatre and a week at L'Odéon in Paris where the audiences were magnificent and just sat in the aisles if there were no seats available. Whether or not they understood every word of Sheridan — it was hard enough in English — I don't know, but judging by the applause they certainly seemed to appreciate it.

We set off for Chicago in April 1986 for their International Theatre Festival, heralding the end of our 12-month run. At the airport, we were having a drink in the departure lounge when Sheila Hancock came in, white as a sheet and looking terrified. She'd seen a man who she was convinced was a terrorist bomber who was going to get on our plane, and she had been following him around the airport to see where he went. It transpired that Sheila was absolutely petrified of flying and had brought along all sorts of hypnotic tapes to help her on the flight. As it happened, we were delayed on the runway because some IRA suspects were being removed from another plane. We also hit some pretty heavy turbulence after we finally took off, so by this time we were all getting pretty nervy. All except Sheila. By now she had forgotten about her 'bomber' and was away with the fairies underneath her headphones!

I had expected Chicago to be a sprawling industrial city with huge chimneys belching out smoke, so was delightfully surprised when we arrived in the middle of a heatwave in a beautiful place set right on the shores of Lake Michigan. It was just like being by the seaside.

Throughout my time with the company, I had given Edward Petherbridge a secret nickname — End of Tetherbridge. He's a lovely chap but it always seemed that at every dress rehearsal he would start up some dramatic argument with the director. I don't know why he always left it until then — I could only assume he had come to the end of his tether — and I thought only a couple of people knew what I called him until Edward chatting conversationally happened to say, 'By the way, I do know what you call me. It's rather good really!'

There was also a lot of vitamin and alternative medicine-taking amongst the younger element of the cast at this time ... not quite the norm it is today. They would come down to breakfast loaded with bottles of pills and potions and compare them lovingly — and the funny thing is that they were the only ones off sick!

Being indisposed, however, didn't deter the lovely Claire Moore, a young actress who was later to take over the star role in *Phantom of the Opera*. In the pageant in *The Critic*,

Claire played Britannia and had to be hoisted up in a basket high over the stage to sing 'Rule Britannia'. However, poor Claire had a slight accident one day, tripping over a kerb and badly hurting her ankle. Undeterred and encased in plaster, she insisted upon being literally bundled into the basket to do her bit.

The American audiences were extraordinary. They were very warm but would just wander in late or walk out half-way through — not out of disapproval, but from the mere fact that they had about six engagements to go to that night and were determined to fit them all in! We were often invited after the show to these bashes held by various charities or department stores but by the time we'd arrived in our everyday clothes, having been dressed up on stage all night, the heavily evening-gowned, bejewelled Americans would have eaten everything, and weren't particularly interested in who we were anyway.

When we first arrived at one of our venues, the Blackstone Theatre, we were met by a rather surly backstage crew. Apparently, a British rock band had been playing there and had not been too popular with them for various reasons. But throughout the run, they gradually thawed out and on the last night they formed a sort of guard of honour and applauded us as we came off stage! We had broken all box-office records at the Blackstone and it was decided to hold a farewell party at the John Hancock Tower. A couple of American firms who had been sponsoring the festival offered to pay towards the party, and the company manager John Rothenberg decided to get in touch with the National to see if they would chip in, too, as we had done so well for them. A negative reply came back. They said that as the company had taken tea with Sir Peter Hall before we left that would be their only contribution.

That just about sums up the National for me. I had a good year with them — but I was glad when it was over.

However, a very different sort of national theatre is one of my very favourite venues. That's Theatr Clwyd, hailed as the National Theatre of Wales.

Situated in the unlikely setting of the North Wales market town of Mold, this lovely theatre is perched on a hill and surrounded by fields. It's the only time I've ever been able to look out of a dressing room window and see sheep!

Theatr Clwyd first came to my attention in the early Nineties when I was asked to play hen-pecked husband Henry Hornett in *Sailor Beware*. Playing my wife, the formidable Emma Hornett, was Jane Freeman, Ivy from *Last of the Summer Wine*, along with her telly co-star Kathy Staff, better known as Nora Batty, playing her sister Edie. Directing it was the wonderful Peter James with whom it was great to be working again as he had directed me in the doomed *Thark*. We had a sell-out run and went back there later for the sequel, *Watch It, Sailor* — this time *On the Buses* star Anna Karen played my wife — but it was not quite the success that *Sailor Beware* had been.

The pay was pretty bad, it being a subsidised theatre, but I was always happy to go there if there was nothing more lucrative in the offing because Chester was only half-an-hour's drive away and in rehearsal time I could be guaranteed to get off to see a couple of football matches. Added to that, I had made firm friends with most of the theatre staff, especially Andrew Gordon who was originally our company manager, and I'd found a little hotel, the Bryn Awel nearby, where Terry and Heather Lally who ran it with their family made it like a second home.

Later, I went back to Theatr Clwyd to do *August* with Sir Anthony Hopkins on stage and attend the film's Royal Première there.

Another favourite theatre — for very different reasons — is the Chichester Festival Theatre. I have done two seasons there and when I was asked to do the first play *Hobson's Choice*, with Leo McKern, I jumped at it. I had just moved to Worthing which meant I was only about 30 minutes from home. Wonderful! I learnt a lot more about trap-doors than I ever thought I would doing *Hobson's Choice*. I was playing cobbler Tubby Wadlow and my first entrance was through the trap door. Graham Turner (now in *Where the Heart Is*) was playing Willie Mossop. In our roles, we both worked 'downstairs' which, in our case, was under the stage and we decided from the start to become firm friends as on the ladder to the trap we had to spend a considerable time with our noses up each other's bottom!

Surgical Spirit star Nichola McAuliffe was playing Maggie Hobson and she had a wicked sense of humour. On stage, she had to bang her foot on the trap door to summon us but then instead of standing back when it opened she would deliberately stand with her legs either side of the gap so our first sight was a bird's eye view of her knickers!

We took the play on tour after Chichester where I learned about other trap-doors — some you had to climb over enormous heating pipes to get to, others had ladders so rickety that Graham and I used to hang on to each other for dear life — and then we took it to the Lyric, Shaftesbury Avenue. Leo, who made a marvellous Hobson, had already said he only wanted to stay in the run for a couple of months so his part was taken over by my old mate Frank Thornton.

Much as I was sad to see Leo go, I was rather relieved in a way when Frank came, as being younger and more agile he got through the part much quicker and I never had to worry about missing my train home to the coast!

I was delighted to be linking up with the lovely Sheila Hancock again on my next Chichester season. This time it was Lionel Bart's *Lock Up Your Daughters* with George Cole playing the corrupt judge Squeezum and Sheila playing his wife. I, as usual, was playing a mad old retainer called Faithful! As a prop, they made the mistake — or otherwise as it turned out — of giving me an ear trumpet. Anybody who knows my work will know I will make the most out of anything and the ear trumpet certainly worked wonders this time.

On the opening night, the audience were very slow and we were desperate for some reaction. At one point in the play, I was supposed to fling the ear trumpet, which I had on a string round my neck, back in exasperation. I did, and much to my astonishment and to the astonishment of everybody else on stage, it landed firmly on my head on top of my powdered wig. There was a moment's stunned silence and then the audience erupted into laughter ... and so did we!

After the show, the director Stephen Rayne said, 'I've been told it's wise not to work with children, animals — or Hugh Lloyd with a prop!' But we kept it in although every night as I swung my ear trumpet around I could never be sure where it was going to land next! Faithful was only a small part but I was told by the director to go out there and get a laugh. Which I did.

And all I can say is, thank God for a funny face ... and an ear trumpet!

10

One Glorious August

It was like a dream come true that summer of 1994. The weather was absolutely perfect with not a cloud in the sky, I was in my beloved North Wales ... and all this I was getting paid for! It all started when my agent at the time, Kenny Earl, phoned me to say he had received a fax from Sir Anthony Hopkins in the States asking if I would consider playing a part in a film which was to be his directorial début. I was just about to book my airline ticket when I discovered I would not be going to Hollywood ... but to North Wales, to a tiny seaside resort on the Lleyn Peninsula called Abersoch. To me, this was even better. Kenny's call was followed only minutes later from one by Tony himself, ringing from Los Angeles. He explained that he would be directing and starring in the movie which was to be called *August* and was based on Chekhov's *Uncle Vanya* but set in Wales. After making the film, we would do a stage version of it at Theatr Clwyd. All my favourite places — it sounded too good to be true!

I was to play a character called Pocky, so called because he had pock marks all over his face, who played the mouth organ and was a sort of sponger on the family in the big house. Also pencilled for the film were Leslie Phillips, playing Alexander Blathwaite, Gawn Grainger, playing Michael Lloyd, and Kate Burton, Richard Burton's daughter, who lives in the States was flying over to take the part of Helen.

Abersoch is a beautiful little resort, nicknamed the 'Cowes of the North' as it is a haven for water sports of all kinds, and it was also a haven for the ladies of the company who discovered a wonderful discount designer shop called Alcatraz and spent most of their time saying, 'But it would have cost at *least* three times as much in London,' seemingly to justify their almost daily shopping sprees. All the cast, including Kate who had arrived with her son Morgan and nanny in tow, were staying at the Riverside Hotel, a lovely place run by John and Wendy Bakewell who fed us all on home-cooked Welsh produce and made their own delicious ice-cream in all flavours for everybody.

Our arrival was regarded with obvious interest — and some suspicion — by the locals who wondered what these theatricals would do to their resort.

However, when it became apparent that we were

mostly more than happy to mix in — patronising their local pubs and shops — they soon became very friendly with us.

Our location was a couple of miles away on a sprawling estate called Nanhoron. The family who occupied the house had moved upstairs and the exterior and ground floor were restored perfectly to capture the period.

On our first day there, we all piled into one of Granada Films' minibuses and went up to see it. Caravans, catering marquees and lorries littered the once peaceful site.

'Good God,' exclaimed Tony. 'What on earth have I done?'

There wasn't much time to reflect on that and it was almost dinner time! Tony is absolutely crazy about Indian food ... I think he would eat it for breakfast. Somehow, out there in the middle of nowhere he had found an Indian restaurant, which looked more like a stately home from the outside, set deep in the woods. They had laid on a banquet of curries for us but were open for business as usual as well, although how anybody ever found the place I have no idea. After a while, a couple with two young children came in and sat at a nearby table. Suddenly I noticed the father staring at me, then at Leslie and finally his gaze rested on Tony and his eyes nearly popped out of his head! After all, you'd hardly expect to find a Hollywood film star in the middle of a North Wales forest eating a curry! Tony noticed and turned his head away and the man looked away very embarrassed. But seconds later, Tony turned round again with a great beam on his face ... and sporting a pair of plastic fangs that he used to carry around with him in his pocket as a memento of *Silence of the Lambs*! The ice was broken and soon the kids were sitting on his knee as he posed happily for photographs.

That was Tony all over. There was no side to him. He was Sir Anthony to no one, but Tony to everyone, and he would far rather sit with the crew at mealtimes than with any big-time film executives discussing business.

Filming was great fun, but hard work, as it inevitably meant a long time hanging around in a caravan waiting to be called. The mornings started very early and the day ended pretty late usually. The guys who looked after the caravans and film equipment and acted as permanent on-site security were terrific and ran backwards and forwards with cups of tea for us. One of them heard that I liked salted popcorn as I had been told it was less fattening than crisps which I adore, and on one of his weekends off he returned with an enormous black sack for me, full of popcorn. It was about a year's supply and I hadn't the heart to tell him I had to throw most of it away as I had no room at the hotel to put it anywhere. He had apparantely gone to his local cinema manager and demanded he have this popcorn for a famous star!

On the first weekend off, these poor guys had an awful shock. Sunday had been allotted as the day off from filming and they set off eagerly to find the nearest local for a well-deserved pint. Alas, no one had told them that this tiny part of Wales was still dry on a Sunday. You couldn't even buy booze in the supermarket. Of course, we were all OK as we were in hotels who did not have to adhere to this somewhat archaic ruling. But after that short, sharp shock, the day off was then changed to a Saturday! Of course, Tony hasn't touched a drop stronger than mineral water in over 20 years, but it doesn't stop him being the life and soul of the party and he certainly makes sure other people have whatever they want.

His wife Jenni, a lovely lady, came down to visit a couple of times, but a more regular visitor was his mother Muriel who lives in South Wales. Muriel is a tiny, sprightly lady, who has been nicknamed by some The Empress of Wales, and proud though she is of Tony she can boss him around fiercely when she wants to. I suspect she's the only person who can!

Our Saturday off was very precious to us having worked so hard and long, but Tony with his little boy enthusiasm at being behind the camera as well as in front of it for once just wanted to go over ideas all the time. So I must admit the majority of us would hide in our hotel rooms or take a drive miles out to escape him, while Tony wandered forlornly around the hotel looking for someone to play with.

However, it certainly wasn't all work with him. I, fortunately, had not actually had to play my mouth organ, only learning to look as though I knew how to play it. But Tony, being a great musician — he also wrote all the music for *August* — would often take the instrument out in a crowded place and give an impromptu performance. Among his other talents — the list is endless — is a great gift for mimicry. He could do perfect impersonations of us all and at one point we suggested that we all go home — he could do the voices and employ glove puppets!

We were sad to leave Abersoch, the sea and the sunshine and the friendly community but we were scheduled for a couple of weeks' break before we started rehearsing for the stage version which we were to perform at Theatr Clwyd.

Of course, it was sold out before we even got there. It was lovely to be back at Theatr Clwyd, even if the money was in sharp contrast to what we were paid for the film. Still, we consoled ourselves with the fact that even Tony was on exactly the same money as the rest of us ... theatrical knight of the realm or not!

It was good to be back in the dressing rooms overlooking the fields again but it wasn't so great for Tony who had to keep his curtains drawn the entire time as female fans had taken to creeping along the grass verge that ran outside his window in the hope of catching a glimpse of their idol in his underpants! Tony was very good with the fans and happily signed autographs every night at the stage door, but one night he returned a lady's handshake ... and she promptly fainted!

There was also a bit of excitement backstage at this time. It was no secret that Gawn Grainger, who had been a widower for some time, had been seeing actress Zoe Wanamaker. Gawn's dressing-room, by the way, which was next to mine, had been done out like a 'whore's boudoir' as he described it. He had bought a rug from Mold market, sprayed it with Chanel No 5 and had an enormous romantic-looking portrait of himself on the wall.

One Saturday night, he said he was having the extravagance of a car to drive him back to London. We didn't think much of it at the time until the Monday when we read the papers. He and Zoe had got married ... and he arrived back in time for the show with his new bride in tow, not having breathed a word to any of us!

It was Gawn who was also despatched to a little French restaurant in the high street to make a rather special booking. Theatre impresario Duncan Weldon had announced he was coming to see the show and bringing with him none other than Raquel Welch who was over in the UK to appear in one of his plays.

Gawn went into the restaurant to make a dinner booking for that night. He told the manager, 'There will be Sir Anthony Hopkins, an entrepreneur called Duncan Weldon who gets the bill ... oh, and Raquel Welch.'

The manager roared with laughter. Sir Anthony, yes ... after all, he was just up the road ... but Raquel Welch? Gawn just shrugged. He said the man's face was a complete picture when she actually walked in.

The stage hands had been waiting, tongues hanging out, for a glimpse of her ... but they ended up rather disappointed. A tiny figure, those famous attributes were well hidden underneath a bulky sheepskin coat she had on to guard against the North Wales cold. She came round to see us all and thanked me for my performance. I told everyone that was before she'd even seen me on stage! They stayed overnight at nearby Saughton Hall, a very posh stately hall hotel, where Tony was also staying. The rest of us couldn't afford it.

While we were playing Theatr Clwyd, *Silence of the Lambs* was shown on television. Knowing the lady who ran the place would be on her own that night, and having been informed by her that she was going to watch it, Tony's mischievous sense of humour took over. As it came to the gruesome line where Hannibal Lecter is describing how he cuts out his victim's liver and eats it, Tony rang the woman and repeated the words at exactly the same time! The poor woman nearly fainted, even though she knew it was only Tony.

It was marvellous working with Tony on stage. He's a very generous actor, loves comedy and was all for me getting as many laughs as I could.

In one of the many little notes he used to write to me and the others, he offered, 'Have a laugh and don't spare the prat-falls or the trips.' Seeing him work on stage was a revelation. He would be going through a highly-charged dramatic scene, drunk and weeping. And then come off and say, 'How's your football team doing, Hugh?' There was none of this carrying on the character off stage nonsense with him.

Tony had no interest in any sport whatsoever and I drove him mad by pleading for time off from rehearsals to go and see Chester play. And he always made sure they finished in time for me to get to a match. I think he was glad to get rid of me by then.

We were, by the end, talking about taking it into the West End for a short run but it would have had to have been without me as I had been booked for pantomime and had already missed some rehearsal time as it was. And without me, Tony refused to go. He said it would not be the same without his original team. I felt guilty at the others losing their chance but it was something that had been booked far in advance and Tony was standing firm.

We finished our run at the New Theatre, Cardiff, with the same fantastic audiences. It was sad to say goodbye to what had been such a happy family — but that's always the same away from home with a show.

All in all, it had been a magical summer and autumn and I knew I would always treasure the memories of that glorious *August*.

We were all to meet up twice again, however. Once at Tony's sixtieth birthday bash held at — where else — an Indian restaurant called the Bombay Brasserie, and also for the première of the film.

As Tony is very much involved in the Snowdonia Trust of which Prince Charles is a patron, His Royal Highness agreed to come to the première, which was fittingly held at Theatr Clwyd.

We were to be ferried to the première in a 'fleet of limousines'. However, it's hard enough to get a taxi in Mold so you can imagine limousines are a bit thin on the ground. However, they managed to rustle up two which went backwards and forwards to the hotel in quick succession trying to look like a fleet. I shook hands with the Prince of Wales in the line-up before the film and he did a double-take when he saw me and asked me if I was playing one of the 'heavies'. I'm not quite sure what he meant by that. I told him I was playing a man with spots and he replied, 'There are some excellent cures for those these days I understand.' Perhaps he, too, suffers from the odd pimple! My wife Shân, who has written this book with me, had been with me in Abersoch and Theatr Clwyd and was greatly excited about the royal do. But when we came to take our seats in the theatre that had been converted into a cinema we found ourselves almost in the back row. Shân was horrified, saying, 'You're one of the stars. How dare they shove you at the back.' She went on and on, threatening complaints to the very top ... until a spotlight picked out His Royal Highness and Tony, who made their way up the stalls ... to sit in the very row we were sitting in. I didn't hear a peep out of Shân after that.

It was back in 1978 when Shân Davies, a scatty, blonde-haired Fleet Street tabloid journalist came into my life.

No, I wasn't being pursued by the paparazzi. I was just having a quiet drink one night in Joe Allen's in the Strand with a businessman friend of mine, John Jayes, who drank in my local pub, the Plough at East Sheen.

At the time, I was appearing in the long-running comedy *No Sex Please — We're British* at the Strand and I'd invited John, a very flamboyant, likeable character, and his lady along to see the show.

Afterwards, we'd gone to Joe Allen's and, while we were chatting, the waiter came over and handed John a piece of paper. The message on it read: 'OK, so ignore me while you're with your famous friends.' The waiter pointed to another table where three females sat laughing. John burst out laughing and beckoned them over.

That was my first introduction to Shân. I discovered that she lived literally five minutes' walk around the corner from me and also went to the Plough ... but we had never, ever met. It seemed quite extraordinary in a small community — but then I suppose neither of us led what you could exactly call routine lives! We swapped phone numbers. In addition to her home and office ones, she also gave me a list of about ten Fleet Street pubs where she might be found, and we promised to meet up, which we did. We used to meet for lunchtime drinks in the Plough, usually on a Monday, as it was always Shân's day off from the *Sunday People* where she worked as an undercover reporter, covering some of the most extraordinary stories. She would arrive to tell me of a host of hilarious adventures from the previous week — and I was her captive audience. There was a 30-year age gap between Shân and myself — she was in her twenties and I was in my fifties — but if other people noticed it, we certainly didn't.

We found that we just adored being in each other's company and made each other laugh a lot. On a serious side, we'd also listen to each other's problems. When I met Shân, I was living alone as Carole had moved out some time before.

After a while, the Monday drinks turned into Sunday ones as well and gradually we began to see more and more of each other. This was all over a five-year period but at the beginning of the Eighties it was becoming evident that what we felt for each other was more than just a fun friendship. We really felt we were soul mates.

Eventually, it seemed natural that she should move into my flat — as she hardly seemed to spend any time at hers anyway. I had always said I had no intention of marrying again and Shân, who was single and a career girl, had harboured no thoughts of wedlock at all. But we suddenly decided it was the natural thing to do. Some people who were sceptical said, 'Why don't you just carry on living together?' But it just wasn't for us. We wanted to be together — man and wife.

It was no problem breaking the news to Shân's family. Over the years I had known her, I had got to know her family, too, and I got on with them like a house on fire. They were all as mad as she was, after all! The only problem was breaking the news to the newspapers. It was not that we had anything to hide, just that we wanted to do it in what we thought was the right way and the right time — and we knew all too well what tabloid newspapers were like, of course. And Shân had said firmly that she rather thought she ought to give the exclusive story to her own newspaper or she'd be given the worst possible jobs at work as revenge. Our only worry was whether it might leak to another paper, so in confidence she told her News Editor David Farr who agreed to keep everything quiet until she was ready.

However, of course, these things don't always go to plan. One day, I was home alone while Shân was at work when the phone rang. It was Tim Ewbank from the *Sun*.

Introducing himself, he said, 'What are you up to these days, Hugh? What are you working on?' I knew he had not the slightest bit of interest in what I was doing showbusiness-wise — the story had obviously got out.

After a bit of meaningless chatter about showbusiness, he eventually got around to it.

'Hugh, I hear you're co-habiting with one of our lady Fleet Street colleagues.'

I replied cheerily, 'Oh — you've heard about me and Jean Rook, have you?'

There was a silence and a splutter at the other end of the receiver. But after he had recovered, he started asking me all sorts of questions which made it obvious he knew all about us.

Primed by Shân in advance in the event of this sort of thing happening, I found myself saying parrot-fashion over and over again, 'No comment.'

Eventually, we said our goodbyes.

When Shân got in that evening, I greeted her with the news. 'They're on to us from the *Sun*.' She went white. She, who had been out all day chasing dirty vicars or promiscuous politicians, absolutely filled with rage. And she uttered the most amazing statement for a tabloid journalist.

'How dare people pry into other people's private lives!'

When she had calmed down and admitted to being the most horrendous hypocrite ever, we decided the best thing to do was to call him back and give him the full story. He was going to print something anyway so he might as well get the facts right.

The following morning the Page Three lead carried the headline: TELLY'S HUGH TO WED GIRL HALF HIS AGE. There was a picture of me, but not of Shân. But the story was right next to a picture of the usual topless Page Three model, and people were ringing me up to ask if she was the one I was marrying!

As well as that, when I went down to the main road later to do some shopping, I found I was being hooted at by lorry drivers waving copies of the paper out of the window and shouting, 'Cheers, Hugh!'

After all the furore had settled down — Shân didn't get the sack as her office were very understanding, being used to stealing stories from other papers themselves — it was time to start planning the wedding.

We had decided on a quiet wedding at Richmond Register Office with just a few family and close friends. But the prospective bride's mother Margaret — who hails from the Rhondda Valley — had other ideas.

One night shortly afterwards, she arrived at our flat armed with a list of guests she and my prospective father-in-law Jack had decided to invite.

The list was made up of a variety of 'aunts' and 'uncles' from all over Wales, members of their Welsh Chapel in Clapham Junction and an assortment of people whose children's weddings Shân's parents had attended.

We had to surrender gracefully. There is nothing as distressing as the sight of a prospective mum-in-law's sad expression when you try to put your foot down. And Shân's dad always loves a good knees-up. So I decided — in for a penny, in for a pound. I might as well invite the whole of the Richard Stone Agency which then represented me and consisted of quite a few agents, some of my showbusiness friends and some of my friends from my home town of Chester, including my dear friend Eddie Crewe, who was to be my best man, and his wife Rita — a lifelong friend.

And Shân decided her guest list might as well include the entire staff of the *Sunday People*, which was not an insignificant number! Of course, she realised it might be quite difficult for them to attend on a Saturday but she was determined to issue an open invitation anyway.

We had decided to hold the reception in a marquee in the garden of Shân's parents' home, which was also in East Sheen, and about two or three miles from the Register Office. Our Greek friends at our local wine bar said they'd do the catering and our dear friend Kerry de Courcy said he would supply all the champagne and drive us to the Register Office in his Rolls-Royce.

So far so good. But there was one problem —

Margaret and Jack had told us that many of the guests, especially the maiden aunts who were arriving by train from various far-flung parts of the Welsh Valleys, would be going to their house first and how were we going to get them to the Register Office? We'd have had to hire every minicab in the area! We were discussing this problem with our great friends Roger Mole and John Matthews when they came over one night to see if we were both sane. Roger is a life-long friend of Shân's and John at the time worked as an upholsterer for London Transport.

'What you need,' said John, 'is a bus.' And he knew of a wonderful firm called Obsolete Fleet which hired out vintage buses for such occasions. So we hired one! Kerry said he would put some champagne on board.

And so the great day dawned — Saturday, 23 July 1983. We didn't see the bus until we arrived at the Register Office, by which point nobody was looking at us in the Rolls. They were all gawping at this marvellous old open-top bus with a spiral staircase and a huge sign hanging from it saying 'Shân and Hugh's Wedding Bus'. And, of course, a crowd of passing Saturday shoppers had turned up to stop and stare. One of the guests we had invited was actor Bob Grant from *On the Buses* and when he had heard about our plans to hire the bus he arrived in his jacket and cap from the series over his wedding gear!

Astonishingly, the ceremony went smoothly although I think the poor Registrar was a little fazed by his overflowing room. Shân's sister Lynne and her husband Gwilym were there with their children, and Shân's niece

Bethan and nephew Gareth acted as bridesmaid and pageboy along with little Victoria Kent who is my god-daughter.

The press were out in force when we emerged from the ceremony, but eventually we got ready to set off in the Rolls while everybody else piled on the bus.

We had been a little worried how Welsh chapelites, theatricals and Fleet Street hacks were going to mix together. But we needn't have.

After a couple of glasses of Kerry's champagne on the bus, the maiden aunts were dancing and singing like chorus girls. Shân and I were about the only sober ones by the end of the reception. You just had to take a sip of a drink and someone wanted to talk to you and by the time you'd turned around your glass had disappeared. Still, it was a great success and we both agreed that we were really glad that we hadn't stuck to the original idea of a quiet wedding! We heard later that one of the guests, a rather respectable and quiet bachelor, had fallen through the marquee and given a proclamation that he had decided to come out that he was gay.

Added to that, a married couple from my showbusiness associates were driving back from the reception through nearby Richmond Park. Fuelled with champagne and the romance of it all, they decided to get out and, well, have a 'kiss and cuddle' in the woods. Unfortunately, they had no idea the park gates were about to close and they were discovered by the rather bemused Parks Police Patrol, who were very good about it. After the explanations as to where they'd been, the Parks Police drove the couple's vehicle to the gates, and took them there in their own car and suggested they got a taxi home — and came back for their car the next day, which they did. Of course, Shân and I had no idea about all this until later. We had already departed on our 'mystery' honeymoon.

We could only manage one night away at the time and I had kept it all a secret from her, although I had hinted we might be going to Margate, which is honestly where she thought I was going to take her. We set off in a hired car, festooned, of course, with the usual tin cans, and the route was no problem as Shân has no sense of direction whatsover. Her face was a picture when we drew up outside the Ritz. I had discovered that the manager of the hotel used to manage a hotel in Chester and he provided us with a sumptuous suite overlooking Green Park.

The consequence of this bright idea was that, after quaffing a glass of the champagne that had been waiting for us, Shân discovered there was a phone in every single room. She spent a good part of our wedding night phoning up her mother and various friends saying, 'I'm phoning from the loo ... hang on, I'm ringing from the bathroom now!'

Well, all that was a few years ago now ... although sometimes it seems like only yesterday. Shân and I are due to celebrate our nineteenth wedding anniversary in July 2002. Not bad for a marriage that we know many thought would not last six months! Of course, there have been ups and downs — what relationship doesn't have them? But I think it goes to show that, if you'll pardon the old cliché, if you have love, then it can conquer all.

11

Screen Play

Probably the most important lesson I learned about appearing on screen was back in 1950 when I made my first ever television appearance in the *Centre Show*.

It was broadcast live from the Nuffield Centre in South Adelaide Street in London, which was also the base for weekly entertainment of the troops and I was terribly nervous. Steve Race did the music and the programme was compèred at the time by Frank Thornton who asked me why I was so jittery.

I said, 'It's the thought of all those millions of people watching *me*!'

He replied, 'Just think of it as *one* person watching you and you'll be OK.'

I did — and I was! And it's something I've always adhered to when appearing on TV.

Of course, radio was still more popular in those days and not everybody could afford a television set. Two years before the *Centre Show* I had made my first radio broadcast on the *Stay at Home* show which came from Sale Lido in Cheshire.

This had been pre-recorded and much to my horror and embarrassment my mother invited all the neighbours round to our house to listen to it. I just couldn't stand it and had to go out of the room.

I also did a *Saturday Night Music Hall*, a programme I had stayed in to listen to avidly every weekend when I was a teenager.

But telly was becoming the in thing in our business and five years after my first appearance I had a part in the sitcom *Great Scott — It's Maynard!*, with a cast that included Bill Maynard, Terry Scott, Pat Coombs and Shirley Eaton.

I was playing an Indian chief and had to say the immortal word 'Ugh!' as Indian chiefs do, several times! This got great laughs and eventually Bill, who was playing a scout or a cowboy or something, got quite put out about it.

He wanted to know why *he* couldn't say 'Ugh!' and get the same sort of laughs. It took the director quite a long time to explain that he was on the other side and that cowboys didn't say 'Ugh!'

But the episode that stands out most in my mind is the last one. We'd decided to have a party after the show, and to ensure there was no lack of female company, the writers were given strict instructions to write six girls into the episode so that they'd be around for the festivities afterwards! After that, I started to do lots of one-line parts and it became more and more apparent that television was going to be my 'thing'.

I was married to Josie, who was a concert pianist, at the time and we were asked to do a summer season with the well-known Falderols that year — 1958 — but we turned it down because we realised that TV was the most important media for me. The trouble is that in television if you're not available right there and then, then they'll just go ahead and ring somebody else.

And so I continued to try and get my face well known. In one particular week I actually did five different shows. These included an appearance on *This Is Your Life* for a boy called Jim Slater with whom I had worked while I was at the Wireless College in Colwyn Bay during the war. Jim was a chronic sufferer of muscular dystrophy and had invented a special chair to help his fellow sufferers.

As I was forever running concert parties at the Wireless College, for my off-screen introduction I had to sing a song I had written then called 'Rufus the Russian'. Fortunately, Jim remembered it, though with a title like that I suppose it would be hard to forget.

One role I had forgotten I was suddenly reminded of on a train just the other day. A man approached me and asked if I was on television and when I said that I was, he replied excitedly, 'Yes, I remember! You used to be Sidcup the Butler!'

I nearly fell off my seat! As that was more than 40 years ago I didn't know whether to be flattered or not. Sidcup the Butler, a role which doesn't usually appear in my list of credits, was a character who made several appearances on *The Malcolm Mitchell Show* to get a few laughs in between guest appearances by people like Matt Munro and music from the Malcolm Mitchell Trio.

The show was directed by Richard Afton, whom I can only describe as being on the slightly immodest side. Our rehearsal room was the usual type — a large room with a stage at the end. The only difference in rehearsals was that Richard Afton insisted on sitting alone in a chair in the middle of the stage while he directed the entire cast who were stuck down on the floor. However, this live show gave many artistes their first break and around this time I was making appearances with showmen like Bruce Forsyth, Bob Monkhouse, Benny Hill, Harry Worth and Eric Sykes.

Of course, my life in television reached a turning point the first time I walked into a Hancock rehearsal room on 7 November 1957. After that followed *Hugh and I* and May 1969 heralded the end of my television partnership with Terry Scott in *The Gnomes of Dulwich.*

From there I went on to make a one-off appearance in the highly popular *'Til Death Us Do Part* when Dandy Nichols was the 'silly old moo' in Alf Garnett's life. And 20 years later I was to return for several appearances in the follow-up series *In Sickness and in Health*, with Carmel McSharry taking the place of the late Dandy Nichols.

That series was particularly memorable because it was

rehearsed and filmed during the World Cup of 1990. Apart from Warren Mitchell, among the cast were Arthur English, Ken Campbell, Eamonn Walker, James Ellis, Harry Fowler and John Bluthal and, of course, Alf Garnett's creator Johnny Speight was always around.

If you hadn't watched whatever match was on the night before, you were a virtual outcast in the studio or the canteen. Well, there was just nothing else to talk about and if you hadn't seen the game you just didn't have anything to contribute to the conversation.

So I made sure I saw every match (much to my wife's delight) just so that I wouldn't feel left out. Well, that's my excuse.

Talking of formidable ladies, the larger-than-life Peggy Mount must be queen of them all.

Peggy and I worked together many times and in the early Seventies we had our own series *Lollipop Loves Mr Mole.*

Again, this was written by Jimmy Perry and we played lovey-dovey couple Reg and Maggie Robinson who lived in a cosy cottage in Fulham and called each other by pet names. My brother Bruce, newly arrived back from Africa, was played by Rex Garner and the lovely Pat Coombs was his fragile wife Violet.

Of course, Peggy and I as Reg and Maggie were total opposites, with Maggie being as strong mentally as she appeared to be physically while I was portrayed as 'timidity and kindness personified' — in other words, my trademark hen-pecked husband again! We had various guest appearances from actors who had been in other Jimmy Perry sitcoms — Bill Pertwee from *Dad's Army* and Michael Knowles and John Clegg from *It Ain't Half Hot, Mum*, among them.

One episode was filmed at a safari park where we got mixed up with some lions. Peggy and I had to film a scene were a lion cub had crept up behind us as we sat under a tree. Fortunately, the trainer wasn't far away.

But another shot was done with Peggy and I and Pat and Rex all sitting inside a car in the park ... with lions crawling all over it. There was no sound being recorded in the car, just the expressions on our faces and when it was screened we could quite clearly see Pat, in genuine terror, mouthing a four-letter word which would *not* have been acceptable on our screens 30 years ago!

A few years later I'm proud to say I created and starred in my own series *Lord Tramp*, a children's sitcom.

I played Hughie Wagstaff, a happy, carefree tramp who suddenly finds he has inherited a title, a fortune, a big estate and a 50-room mansion with staff. However, in true Beverly Hillbillies style, he's not sure he prefers this lifestyle to his previous one.

Joan Sims played the housekeeper Miss Pratt and George Moon and Lally Percy were in the regular cast, along with guest appearances from Leslie Dwyer and Jack Watling, Alfie Bass and Aubrey Woods.

But although it was all my own creation I didn't always have a say in what happened, which is why on one occasion I found myself in the loneliest place in the world as far as

I'm concerned — sitting on a horse with no saddle or reins and facing its tail! Anybody who has had to suffer this, staring at a horse's backside while the director wants numerous takes, will know what I mean! I always enjoy doing children's television and once made an appearance in Stanley Baxter's *Mr Majeika* which was about a wizard sent to England from the planet Walpurgis.

I've always said that, as an actor, as you get older you don't retire, you just play older parts. But on this occasion I think I really reached my limit. I played a 500-year-old wizard! I had a wonderful costume — a long robe which was made to look absolutely filthy as I had supposedly landed on Earth by mistake and was wandering around the woods trying to get back to my own planet. But my wig was the crowning glory ... literally.

The wardrobe team had made the most marvellous creation which flowed right down to my waist and was filled with twigs, leaves and birds' nests. We were filming outside near Maidstone in Kent. It was a boiling hot day and, much as I loved my costume and wig, I was looking forward to getting out of them.

My wife Shân had come with me for a day out and we were sitting around in the sunshine just waiting for me to be told I could go. Eventually, I was given the green light and rushed off to start changing when they suddenly called me back.

'Sorry, Hugh,' they said, 'there's a hair in the gate,' which meant there was something wrong with the film.

So I was left with the prospect of sitting around for

ages until they got a call from the lab that all was clear or we had to re-shoot the scene.

When we had arrived at the location, we noticed a little pub just down the lane from where we were filming. Normally, I would not dream of going off set in a costume for fear of damaging it, but in this case if you tipped a gallon of beer over it or burnt it with a cigarette I don't think anybody would have noticed. So, given permission, Shân and I set off down the lane to have a much-needed drink.

It was very quiet and there was hardly a soul around, but I had forgotten that at the bottom of the lane was a main road on which the pub stood. As we approached it, I realised it was quite a busy thoroughfare and a couple of drivers gave me a quick glance ... and then did a double-take, almost crashing into each other! I suppose it's not every day you come across a 500-year-old wizard with waist-length hair when you're driving home from work! I decided we'd better get into the pub quickly before I caused a major pile-up. Fortunately, the landlord knew that we were filming just up the road and didn't bat an eyelid as he poured a well-earned pint.

Another children's series I appeared in was *Woof*, about a boy who turns into a dog from time to time. This one-off appearance turned out to be highly lucrative as I frequently get repeat fees for it from all over the world. It was a highly enjoyable job as my wife was played by the wonderful Jean Alexander, known by millions of *Coronation Street* viewers as Hilda Ogden. (I also really enjoyed working with the dog!) Jean is a delightful, petite and very elegant lady, in stark

Above: A scene from *Hancock's Half Hour* – 'The Lift'. There I am as the lift man himself.

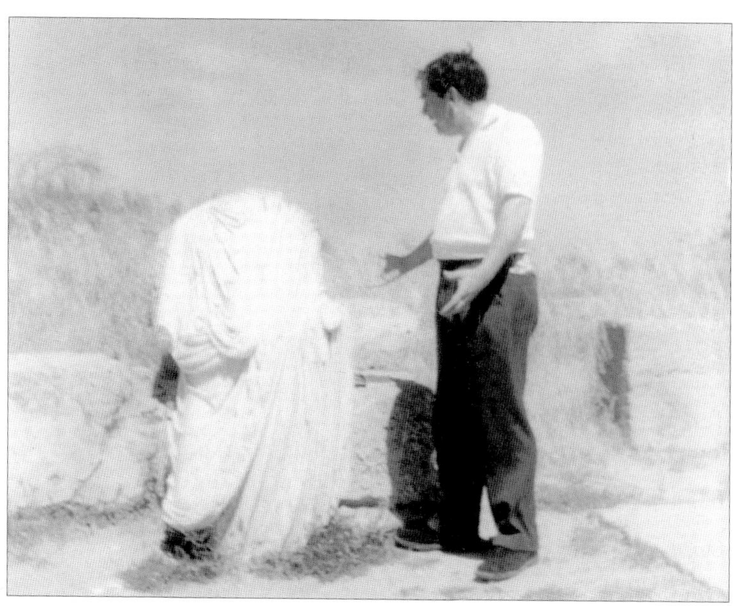

Right: Tony Hancock has a meaningful conversation with a headless statue on Cyprus... taken by me!

As Buttons in *Cinderella.*

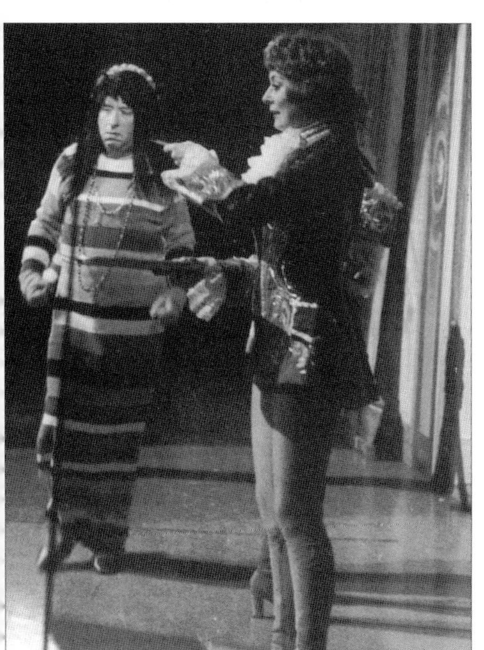

Oh yes he did! Here are a few of my pantomime appearances…

Above: A star-studded Dick Whittington cast: (left to right) me, Anthea Askey, John Hanson, June Whitfield, Roy Hudd, Honor Blackman, Jack Tripp, Richard Murdoch and Allan Christie.

Below left: In panto at the Opera House in Manchester, pictured here with Lizzie Power.

Below right: With Russell Hunter as Ugly Sisters in Manchester.

J. B. PRIESTLEY
KISSING TREE HOUSE, ALVESTON,
STRATFORD-ON-AVON, WARWICKSHIRE.
Stratford-on-Avon 3798

Nov. 14 1970

Dear Hugh Lloyd,

All my best wishes for Tuesday night, and may you have a long and happy run!

I don't know who thought of you to play Herbert S., but it was a piece of inspired casting. Your performance from the first has given me very great pleasure. Many thanks indeed for all that you bring to the play.

Yours sincerely,
J B Priestley

A flattering piece of praise from JB Priestley.

As Arnold Crouch in *Not Now Darling* at the Phillip Theatre, Sydney.

With Susie Blake, in *Hands Across the Sea*, from Noel Coward's *Tonight at 8.30*.

Above: With the cast of The National Theatre Company's production of Chekhov's *The Cherry Orchard.*

Below: With Roy Kinnear and Sir Ian McKellen at the Chicago International Theatre Festival.

Above: On the set of *Dr Who* in Barry Island, South Wales, with producer John Nathan-Turner (centre) and Stubby Kaye.

Below: With Peggy Mount and a lion cub in *Lollipop Loves Mr Mole*.

One of the happiest days of my life: Shân and I get married at Richmond Registry Office.

Above: Shân and I at a Concert Artistes Association Ball.

Below: With the Chester City 'Famous Five' (from left to right) Elfed Morris, Micky Metcalf, Hugh Ryden, Gary Talbot and Jimmy Humes. These five were forwards who scored twenty goals each in the 63/64 season.

Up The Blues!

Above: In training with the lads! Me with the Chester City Football Squad and, *below left*, in goal.

Below right: Me as a ball sponsor, with Lynne Williams, match sponsor for Chester City Football Club at Deva Stadium.

A still from the film *White Cargo*, with David Jason and Tim Barrett.

contrast to her screen character. When we first bumped into each other in the hotel bar, she seemed quite breathless. It transpired that she had been up and down the corridors memorising the fire exits, the first thing she did when she arrived at a hotel, she said. Very sensible when you come to think of it. Far more sensible than most of us who just headed straight to the bar for a large drink.

Still in the world of make-believe, I also made an appearance in the legendary *Doctor Who* series as a Welsh bee-keeper called Goronwy! Even now, I get fan letters from people all over the country who remember me for that role alone.

I played the part in an episode called *Delta and the Bannerman* produced by my good friend John Nathan-Turner. We filmed it at a disused holiday camp at Barry Island in South Wales and I actually had to wear the full bee-keeper's gear — straw hat and veil — and deal with a hive full of real bees. Fortunately, a real bee-keeper was on hand to make sure I didn't get stung.

Doctor Who was great fun to work on. John always created a wonderful atmosphere for the cast, who in this instance included Sylvester McCoy as The Doctor, Bonnie Langford as his assistant and a wealth of star names including Stubby Kaye, Don Henderson and Ken Dodd.

On this particular occasion, I had taken along our young pointer puppy Deva, named after the Roman name for Chester. John's own dog, Pepsi, who had made appearances in many television series, was also there. But whereas Pepsi, a cross chow, was a grand old lady of about

15, Deva was a neurotic, hyper-energetic puppy of six months who just wanted to play, so it caused a bit of havoc on location, especially for the long-suffering floor manager Gary Downie who kept having to shout through his loud-hailer, 'Will someone get those bloody dogs off the set?!' Filming can be a long, arduous business — but it can also be a lot of fun.

I was delighted to be asked to play the part of a drunken butler called Selfridge in David Croft and Jimmy Perry's hit series *You Rang, M'Lord.*

As most of the cast had been in their previous success, *Hi-de-Hi,* by now they had produced T-shirts proclaiming 'Where Will It All End?' They were just like one big family. For one episode we were all based in Norfolk where we stayed in a local hotel. After a long day's filming, plenty of refreshment was taken in the bar and by midnight Su Pollard was usually trying to get people to go with her and ring on doorbells and run away! On one occasion, we were doing a night shoot at an enormous mansion out in the Norfolk countryside. The house was owned by a man called Robin Coombes who was the Coombes of Watney Coombes Reid, the brewers. The grounds were fantastic with a lake running through the gardens and tame otters basking by the banks.

On the night we were filming, the family were holding a dinner party in their home. We, of course, had our caterers on site and tucked into a barbecue as the dinner guests — including Tory MP Gillian Shepherd, then hotly tipped for the Cabinet, and actor Stephen Fry's parents — arrived and quaffed pink champagne on the terrace.

We were still eating after they had gone inside to dine and someone jokily suggested that Bill Pertwee, who was dressed as a policeman, gatecrash the gathering and arrest some guests for allegedly nicking the silver. Su Pollard, who was kitted out in her usual housemaid's costume, needed no second bidding.

The windows to the dining room came right down to ground level so, grabbing Bill by the hand, she pulled up the window and they both climbed in and duly carried out the joke.

We gathered there was a mixed reaction from some of the guests as these 'strange actor chappies' barged into their dinner party. But as for Robin Coombes, a lovely man, he was delighted.

'I'll dine out on this one for months!' he said.

I loved playing the part of the drunken butler. To play a drunk you should always underplay it, not overact it. But I must admit I had a worrying moment when I realised I had a scene where I was actually supposed to be *sober*! I'd never played the character in anything but his cups, so it took me quite a while to work out how he'd behave without a drink!

And while we're on the bottle, I was once in a series called *The Bottle Boys*, all about milkmen, which starred *Confessions* actor Robin Asquith.

In one scene, I was supposed to be sitting on the high ledge of a block of flats, threatening to jump off. As I get dizzy sitting on a cushion, I asked my agent to ask them if I would really have to be high up.

The production staff were most concerned and said no,

of course not. It would all be done in the studio.

When I arrived to film the scene, I found my high ledge was about two inches off the ground. And even then they were worried in case that was too high for me! In complete contrast, I have never been able to sleep lying flat on my back with one, or no pillows. I always have to be propped up and this cost me a job in *Casualty*.

They wanted me to play a heart-attack victim but it meant I would have to lie flat with no pillow on a hospital bed. I had to turn the job down. I told them I was sorry but that I probably *would* have a heart-attack if I had to lie like that while they did take after take!

At around this time, I made an appearance in *Boon* with Michael Elphick. The series was filmed in the Nottingham area and in the episode I was in we were filming a court scene in a disused courthouse. In the middle of shooting, the bells of a nearby church started chiming ... and didn't stop! We discovered it was bell-ringers' practice time and eventually the director asked one of the assistants to go round there and ask them very nicely if they would mind ceasing their pealing while we finished filming.

The assistant went off and duly returned — the bells still ringing. He told the director that he had put the request very politely and they had replied equally politely that they would be happy to stop ringing the bells if the film unit would make a donation to their church fund ... of £20,000! Needless to say, the bells carried on tolling and we had to work the filming around them.

Although I thoroughly enjoyed my one-off parts in so

many series, I was delighted to have appeared in three Alan Bennett television plays — *Say Something Happened* with Dame Thora Hird and Julie Walters; *Me, I'm Afraid of Virginia Woolf*; and *A Visit from Miss Protheroe* with Patricia Routledge.

The latter was directed by the creative Stephen Frears who hadn't been in the studio very much as he had been doing outside camera shots. When it came to filming in the studio, there was a very heavy fireplace which was part of the scenery and it had to be moved around all the time by the crew for him to take shots from different angles.

After it had been moved for the umpteenth time, one of the cameramen was heard to remark wryly, 'I remember the day when the camera used to move.'

I can never resist changing scripts if I feel they need it but I met my match with Alan Bennett. A few times I suggested to him that we change a word or a line and he would say he would go away and think about it. He always returned saying diplomatically that he thought perhaps his phrase was the correct one.

And, of course, he was always right, being such a brilliant wordsmith. Added to that, he's the only author who has bought me a bottle of champagne for my performance!

Although people normally associate me with comedy, I have done quite a few serious dramas. One was *A Matter of Will* with Brenda Bruce. It was an almost exclusively female cast and I spent all the time in rehearsal trying to follow the conversation on knitting patterns and flower arranging. It was all set around a romance in a nursing home and I found myself back in a nursing home again for a BBC Scotland TV play called *The Dunroamin' Rising*. In this I played the part of an old boy who could only communicate by whistling and had to learn to whistle everything from 'Jerusalem' to 'Danny Boy'. This was a bit startling for my fellow residents in the hotel in Glasgow where we were housed as I started practising at 6.00am before going out filming.

It's a wonder I didn't put on about ten stone in the month it took to film the play. On location, the food provided by the 'chuck wagon' is always excellent and it mystifies everybody how these amazing meals can suddenly appear from the back of a not very large van. There's so much hanging about when filming that there's honestly not a lot to do except eat ... to stop getting bored! As soon as you arrive on set, it's bacon butties, followed by elevenses with coffee and biscuits, followed by lunch with a delicious choice of hot meals or salads and puddings, followed by tea with biscuits and cakes, followed by supper if you're still at it. If not, it's bound to be dinner back at the hotel!

On this particular occasion, we were also required to eat large platefuls of mince and tatties while filming, sometimes three times a day in addition to what we were being provided with on set. My wife couldn't understand why I felt duty bound to eat everything provided by the film caterers as well, but it's such a long day you find the food is just something you look forward to to alleviate the boredom.

Also in the play were Scots actor Russell Hunter, best

known for his role as Smelly in the TV series *Callan* and with whom I had played an Ugly Sister in pantomime in Manchester, and the outrageous Thorley Walters, who had all the staff at the hotel running about in a spin. Apart from having rather an eye for the ladies, Thorley always seemed to want to be different. The hotel had a very good à la carte restaurant which Thorley would sit right in the middle of and, having perused the menu and the wine list for ages, would then demand a poached egg on toast and a glass of milk — or if he had fish, as he sometimes did, he would always claim to the staff that it was not fresh, but 'boil in the bag'. But he was a marvellous, larger-than-life character and made everybody laugh.

Food also centred around a very prestigious TV drama I did called *She's Been Away*, where I had to sit in Fortnum and Mason's restaurant and Dame Peggy Ashcroft and I had to hurl bread rolls at each other. The cast also included the distinguished actor James Fox.

And I often got accosted in the supermarket after appearing in a sketch with the marvellous Victoria Wood, with whom I have worked several times, much to my delight. The sketch was in the form of a spoof documentary about an old man and how he exists living alone on his pension — in the end he escapes from the social workers and do-gooders, climbs out of the window and says he's off to Majorca! But one section shows me shopping in the supermarket for 'spaghetti 'oops' which I seemingly live on. For ages after that, people would come up to me and say, 'Have you got your 'oops, Mr Lloyd?' or wave a tin of them at me.

It was great fun doing a recent episode of the revived *Randall and Hopkirk Deceased* series. We filmed part of it in some underground caves which were freezing cold but fortunately my costume was an enormous fur hat and cloak so I was about the only one who kept relatively warm. I had just one word to say — 'Yes' — but by the time we'd finished filming I'd managed to increase that to about six 'Yeses', much to the amusement of Charlie Higson the director who was great to work with, as were the rest of the production team and crew.

The only trouble with film work as far as I'm concerned is all the dressing up, as I generally end up in some elaborate costume which I hate. I know I'm probably unique in the business as far as that goes. So it was pretty awful, although I loved the part, when I appeared in a film production of *Alice in Wonderland*, shown in the States and recently on television in the UK.

It had a cast of thousands, including Gene Wilder, Ben Kingsley, Whoopi Goldberg, Ken Dodd, Sheila Hancock ... the list was endless.

I played a fish-faced footman and, to my disgust, had not only to put on the footman's uncomfortable costume but I had to be painted blue and silver as well. The things I suffer for the sake of my art! It's a funny old world in film and television but it's one I'm proud of being part of, even though there have inevitably been drastic changes over the years and not always for the better.

I'm constantly being stopped by people who think they know me from somewhere else. I've been mistaken for the insurance man, a former next-door neighbour, someone's distant uncle — a host of different things — until it dawns on them: 'You're on the telly!' It opens up a whole world of new friends and acquaintances that you would probably never have spoken to if you hadn't got a familiar face.

For I've been in all their living rooms ... and it's a privilege to be there!

12

No More Shouting at Night

It always amuses me that when I get in the back of a black taxi cab I always seem to get the same remark from the driver.

'Haven't seen you on telly lately, guv'nor. Have you retired?'

When I point out that perhaps I was in two things in the past fortnight and am due to be in an episode of something else in a week or so's time they also always give the same reply.

'Oh, well, in this job with all the hours I work I never get to watch the telly.'

So why they bother to ask in the first place I really don't know.

I certainly have no intention of retiring if I can help it.

I love my work too much — and, anyway, my bank manager won't let me! But what I have given up is what we call in the business 'shouting at night'. That, of course, means treading the boards in the theatre. It's such an antisocial pastime, working six nights a week and matinées — and if it means travelling from my home in Sussex every day up to the West End ... forget it. And, of course, the local subsidised theatres these days get away with paying the actors peanuts for all that work ... I've done it all before, so now I've decided to quit that side of the business.

But, of course, I do love television and film work and, fortunately, up to now there seems to be quite a bit about. And one potentially lucrative area of the business which is often overlooked is the realm of TV adverts.

In the past, I've done quite a few. I have to admit, I don't understand many of today's advertisements — especially the ones for cars. They seem to bear no relevance to the product at all. You might be able to remember the commercial, but I bet there aren't many people who can remember what on earth they were advertising. So what's the point of it all?

In the mid-Sixties, I did three commercials on the trot for Wisdom Toothbrushes. They asked me who I would like to direct them and I immediately said David Croft who had directed me in *Hugh and I* amongst other things and with whom I worked well as he is such a brilliant director.

They had booked the studios for three days but David and I, knowing each other so well, had done one-and-a-half commercials by lunchtime on the first day. This absolutely horrified the advertising people because they were used to having film directors, not television directors, who took a long time to set up the shots. This meant that the advertisers and their clients could have long and expensive lunches every day. So we compromised — and had long and expensive lunches ourselves and dragged it out.

In one of the adverts, I was on a motorbike — but I didn't have to ride it, thank goodness, as it was on a lorry which was attached to a car! Although the adverts were very successful, I wasn't asked to do any more and I think that was because in a well-publicised interview some time afterwards I revealed that I had had false teeth since my teens. Hardly the best advertisement for a toothbrush!

On another occasion, a famous brewery wanted to publicise their new beer bottle and they selected Terry and myself to do their ads. However, they had to choose the time when we were both on holiday — I was at Cap d'Antibes on the French Riviera and Terry was also abroad, so I flew back to London on the Saturday night. The following morning, everybody met up at the Kensington Film Studios with the celebrated director Dick Lester, who was to direct the commercial. He had previously directed me in a Helen Shapiro film in which I had to have custard pies thrown at me. It was supposed to be a one-day job but it ended up taking three days because on the first day they threw the custard pie and it was so hard it nearly knocked me out and it didn't stick to my face! On the second day, they made it so runny that none of it stayed on me; and on the third day, they made it just right but the props men who were throwing it at me off-camera kept missing me! Exasperated by now, Dick Lester said, 'I'll do it myself.' So he did — and he was eventually successful.

As a consequence, when I went to do the beer commercial I was already on good terms with him. So we made four one-minute, off-the-cuff commercials that morning and I was back in Nice — after travelling on an empty Caravelle aeroplane — in time for dinner by 7.30 on Sunday evening. The commercials were shown in Scotland and apparently were quite successful. They were going to network them nationally when they realised they'd changed the shape of the bottle *again* — so that was the end of that!

Still on the subject of beer, Terry and I had another ale commercial for a big poster campaign for a well-known Midlands Brewery. For the photo session, we were handed two foaming pints. I asked them, 'Is it your beer?'

Horrified, they said, 'No! Don't drink it for God's sake, because it's half lemonade, half Coke ... and there are soap suds on the top!'

In 1982, I went to South Africa with a bunch of other actors to make three or four commercials for Qualcast lawnmowers. We flew over there in February, the reason being that the new products came out in March and they wanted sunshine to make them look as though it was almost summer when they would look their best. On our arrival in Cape Town, we were met by the local crew and when we said we had come for the sunshine they told us that this was the first fine day they'd had for a week! The prospects looked good, though, for the following day when the shooting was to start and the scene crew were off early to prepare their first set which was to be the exterior of an English house. Unfortunately, before any filming could start, by 9.30am the set had blown down! So shooting was delayed. We actors didn't mind, of course, because we were all booked there for about ten days anyway, presumably because it was cheaper for the film company to take a block of people over for ten days than one at a time.

In the end, all was well and, during my stay there, I enjoyed the company of the late James Villiers, whose widow Lucy is now one of my agents. I also met up with actor Rex Garner who starred with Peggy Mount, Pat Coombs and me in *Lollipop Loves Mr Mole*. Rex is now a very well-established television star in South Africa. And for the lawnmower ads, I very much enjoyed working with the celebrated film director Cliff Owen. But I'm afraid neither the sunshine nor the lawnmowers did anything to improve my non green-fingered state ... and I don't think I've ever felt the urge to mow a lawn since!

Despite my lack of horticultural expertise, the last commercial I did was for Viscount Biscuits in which I played ... a gardener! It was shot in a lovely stately home which had a fountain spouting water behind me as I sat grinning and munching my way through a packet of Viscount biscuits. I ate far too many of them during the course of the filming ... but I would love to do that particular shoot all over again!

I have turned down a few roles in the past couple of years, though, because there's such a slant towards sex, violence and bad language. I'm no prude but I draw the line with scripts that involve teenage rape and swearing at every other word, even if my particular part isn't involved in those scenes. Throughout my career, I have never been associated with that sort of production and I don't intend to start now. I would never appear in anything that I would be too embarrassed for my family and friends to watch.

But over the last couple of years I have been offered some delightful roles in some really good productions that I have been happy to do.

I'd always wanted to be involved more in films so I was delighted to be asked to be in two Dickens productions — *Great Expectations* and *Oliver Twist* — especially as Charles Dickens is my favourite author.

The former was filmed at Pinewood Studios and starred Ioan Gruffudd, who is a very nice, unassuming Welsh boy, and I was playing the Aged Parent! Our scene was set in a parlour room where I sat wrapped up in the corner while chickens ran all around the set and a pig was also being featured in it.

It was chaos! Unfortunately, when the pig was brought in one of the hens started chasing it and the squealing pig ran straight through a plate glass window which was part of the scenery. As luck would have it, it wasn't hurt at all but the shock drove it hysterical and then the chickens followed suit and went crazy, too, so it took us a bit of time to get that scene shot.

Oliver Twist, however, was being shot in the Czech Republic about 20 miles away from Prague. The reason for this is because the studios are so cheap out there but it seems ridiculous that it's more economical to fly out a whole cast and crew and put them up at top hotels than it is to film it in Britain. Something's wrong somewhere!

For my role as one of the directors of the board who send Oliver to the orphanage, I had to grow side-whiskers. They do offer to stick fake ones on but I find the spirit gum so messy to get off — apart from the fact that you get quite a buzz if you get a whiff of it first thing in the morning!

When I arrived at Heathrow to fly to Prague, I met up with about half-a-dozen of my fellow 'directors of the board' who were also in various stages of growing whiskers.

On arrival at the passport check in Prague, we filed past the unsmiling Czech official one by one and I was the last in line. Of course, our passport pictures looked nothing like any of us as we were all clean-shaven in them, and the uniformed Czech looked at each of us, then at the photos with growing amazement. When it finally got to me, he just took one look ... and burst out laughing.

We were only there for a few days and didn't get to see much of Prague itself, only the hotel, as we left for filming at a disused monastery first thing in the morning and didn't get back to the hotel until late at night. But we had quite a lot of fun on set, despite the fact that it poured with rain most of the time and the ground around our location caravans was like a mud bath.

And it was lovely to be working with the marvellous Liz Smith, now playing the grandma in the brilliant *Royle Family*, and also Julie Walters, one of my favourites who never stops making people laugh on and off screen.

A year or so ago, I was asked to appear in a television adaptation of Laurie Lee's *Cider with Rosie*.

I was to play the part of an ancient rural type (just for a change!) who had fallen on hard, well, impoverished times, reduced to eating potato peelings, and was about to be carried off to the workhouse where he and his devoted wife would be parted for the first time in their lives and subsequently meet an almost instant demise without each other.

The part of my wife was played by a wonderful, sprightly, 90-year-old actress called Katherine Page who had lots of television work lined up.

She told me, 'I'm about the only one left to play the roles they want because everybody else is dead!'

My make-up was incredible — a deathly pallor — and I looked like a walking corpse. Everybody stood back in shock when they saw me. But the funny thing was that I had to go for the obligatory insurance medical that you usually have to undergo before filming, just to make sure you're likely to last the three weeks or so that they need you! It seemed pretty incongruous to be going along for a medical to play somebody who was about to die.

A role that followed was one that I must say I enjoyed enormously — because I had an unexpected bonus to the job. This one was for an episode of the Alan Davis series *A Many Splintered Thing* which was screened recently.

I was only required for one day's filming, a night shoot, in fact.

We were filming in the Kent seaside resort of Margate

and had taken over a bed and breakfast establishment with the unlikely name of the Vienna Guest House.

My role was that of a Welshman who was celebrating his Golden Wedding Anniversary and I only had a short, but very amusing, scene with Alan.

We arrived at the guest house in the early evening where, of course, the crew and lighting boys were already hard at work. Although I was very happy to be working as always, I had been a little disappointed to find that I was missing a live television match in which Manchester United were playing some European side. I'm not interested in watching football on the television unless it's live — for instance, I never watch *Match of the Day* — as I believe that live broadcasts are what television was meant for in the first place. So I was sorry to be missing this opportunity, but work had to come first. We hung around for a bit as the crews sorted out all their cables and cameras and then eventually one of the production guys came up to me and the actress who was playing my daughter and apologised for the delay but said they still had to get a few things sorted out. Added to that, they had decided to shoot another scene before ours but the guest house owner had kindly agreed to let us have one of their bedrooms to sit in so we could have a cup of tea and watch the television until we were needed.

As we entered the room, the players were just walking on to the pitch.

I sat there drinking cups of tea, engrossed in what was a brilliant match, expecting someone to come in at any moment and say that I was needed.

But would you believe it? Just as the final whistle blew, the door opened, a head popped round and said, 'Can you come down now, Hugh?' So I saw the whole match, and I was getting paid for it! And shortly afterwards, I received a very nice letter from the production company, Lucky Dog, thanking me very much for my performance but apologising that they had to keep me hanging around for so long!

After that one, Christmas came early for me last year ... in fact, I celebrated it in September! I was delighted to be asked to play the part of the 'real' Santa Claus in a Christmas Special they were recording of Ardal O'Hanlon's *My Hero* series.

There were a couple of fake store Santas in the Special but I was to be the real thing whom Ardal, as a sort of Superman, flies off to get from the North Pole or wherever.

After rehearsing in London for most of the week, we recorded the Special at the lovely Teddington Studios which has a much more homely feel to it than the bigger television studios.

On the Friday, we were rehearsing during the day and then doing the show before a studio audience in the evening.

At lunchtime, I decided to go to the canteen for a snack and, to my amazement, discovered that the studios had entered into the festive spirit of things and were providing full Christmas dinner — roast turkey with all the trimmings and Christmas pudding! So my snack went by the board and I decided to tuck in to the full works.

Well, after all, I was the real Father Christmas, and if my girth widened a little by the afternoon it would only look more realistic — they'd just have to let the costume out!

While filming at the beginning of 2001, I came across a guy whom I feel represents real comedy as I know it — Lee Evans.

I must confess, I didn't know a great deal about him before, although now I understand he has a cult following, but Lee is an enormously naturally funny person, as well as being a delight to work with.

When the script first arrived asking if I was interested in playing the part of a sort of 'pensioner-conman', I read it — and was rather alarmed.

Although I found it hilarious, my role consisted of being bashed into lamp-posts, dropped on my head and thrown into a skip! Having being firmly reassured by my lovely agents Lucy Villiers and Nancy Hudson that I was guaranteed a stunt double for those bits, I agreed to do it. And I didn't regret my decision for a moment.

It was a laugh-a-minute rehearsing and filming and Lee never ceases to entertain both on- and off-take! But the story behind one of the scenes that will be screened is just as funny as the episode itself. In one scene, I am seen losing my false teeth down a toilet bowl. As I've mentioned before, I've worn dentures since I was a teenager but obviously they weren't expecting me to drop my own set down the lavatory.

So the make-up department asked me for the telephone number of my dentist, who had actually not long previously made me a new set — so they could have a replica set made to chuck down the loo! I thought I had better warn this rather respectable establishment that the BBC might be ringing, and tried explaining to them that we only wanted a new set made (quite a costly business) to throw down a toilet! I don't think they've ever had such a bizarre request, but it certainly seemed to have them in hysterics, although I'm not sure quite what sort.

But the irony of it all was that, of course, the teeth weren't being thrown down a proper toilet anyway — not on a studio set. In fact, the bowl was just full of fresh, clean water, and it would have probably been even more sterile than if I'd stuck them in a glass of Steradent! However, the new dentures were made — at what cost I can't imagine — and still remain as pristine and pure as the day they were created.

As well as my television work, Shân and I have found a new outlet — cruising! But it's not all lying about in the sun, although I must admit it's a wonderful way to have a paid holiday.

For a couple of years, we've been taking to the high seas — or rather, the calm, blue waters of the Mediterranean and the like — taking my life story to the cruisers as celebrity lecturers.

Shân and I do a sort of chat show with her interviewing me about various episodes in my life. I do a few gags, sing the odd song and we have a bit of domestic banter which always goes down well. We've seen some wonderful places, from Bethlehem to the Norwegian fjords, from Africa to Aphrodite's birthplace. We've made some great new friends and I hope given our audiences a few laughs along the way. Because I do like to keep the laughter going.

No More Shouting at Night

I don't watch alternative comedians because I don't really appreciate their humour, but I feel that, with the likes of Ardal O'Hanlon and Lee Evans around, the future of real comedy is secure.

13

True Blue

Some of my happiest childhood memories, from when I was about eight years old, are Saturday afternoons ... and football matches! My dad was not very keen on soccer — or any sport, for that matter — so I used to be taken to the Chester City Football Club matches by 'Uncle' Harry who lived next door. Of course, Dad would always step in if Uncle Harry was unavailable, but I don't think he ever really enjoyed the games. It was always a big event for Uncle Harry to accompany me, because at home he would never put his false teeth in. But on Saturday afternoons he made a special effort in order to take me to the match.

We would walk in all weathers — it didn't matter whether it was snowing or raining or how cold it was —

from our homes in Raymond Street, across the canal and down Whipcord Lane to Sealand Road where the stadium used to be. As there were not many cars around in the early Thirties, the route to the stadium was jam-packed with blue-and-white-scarfed walkers. The average attendance in those days was far more than it is today. It was around 8,000 and there were only two policemen on duty in case of eventualities, which just goes to show how times have changed.

My love for my home-town football club has stayed with me since those early days and I have supported them through thick and thin. I have never felt the slightest urge to change my allegiance to one of the bigger clubs nearby like Liverpool or Manchester United who always seem to be on top. Perhaps that stems from playing the underdog roles all my life!

When, as a teenager, I joined the *Chester Chronicle* as a cub reporter — as I mentioned earlier — I became the Football Correspondent. In those wartime days, many star footballers had joined up, and among those who played for Chester were Scottish International Andy Black, English International Leslie Compton, Bill Pendergast and the legendary Tommy Astbury — all names that soccer fans of my generation will remember well.

Often, the opposition team's reporter couldn't make the game and he would ring me to ask me to do a report for them. So I would end up writing three versions of the same game — one for the *Chester Chronicle*, one for the opposition and one for the Sunday newspapers!

Although I moved away from my home town when I was quite young, I have always managed somehow, wherever in the world I have been, to stay in touch with what's happening at the club. Today, of course, there's the Club Call telephone information service giving the latest news and interviews on line ... you should see our phone bill! And I'm also very friendly with the current Sports Editor of the *Chester Chronicle*, Ian Bedford, and his lovely wife Sheila. We usually chat at least once a week and he lets me know what's going on — or I tell him what I've heard on Club Call! But up until a few years ago, this service didn't exist and I relied solely on word of mouth from friends and fellow fans.

The extent of the soccer grapevine is best illustrated when I arrived in Chicago with the National Theatre Company for the International Theatre Festival. I had left Britain on the day Chester were playing a crucial match, which would decide whether or not they gained promotion to the next division. I was a bit miffed at not being able to discover what had happened and reckoned I'd just have to wait a month until we got back. However, when we arrived in the early hours of the morning at the huge Americana Congress Hotel where we were all staying, we went to check in and I was summoned over by the most enormous hall porter I have ever seen. He said, 'Your name Lloyd?'

Trembling, I nodded, wondering what on earth I had done.

He handed me a slip of paper and said, 'Message for you.'

Written on the piece of paper were just two lines: 'Chester 2 – Lincoln 1.' I couldn't believe my eyes. I knew I was a bit jet-lagged and thought I must be dreaming. What a welcome to Chicago! But to this day, I have no idea who sent the message, or who had even known where we were staying. And nobody has ever owned up to it but it was a delightful way to start the festival.

I try to see Chester play as often as I can and we get up to the city maybe three or four times a year — always in the football season, of course! And if they happen to be playing teams down south, then we may go as well, but it doesn't really have the same atmosphere for me as watching them play in my own home town.

One of the most memorable games I have ever witnessed was in 1964 when Chester played Brighton. Terry Scott — although he was a Watford supporter — and I went along to cheer Chester, and Norman Wisdom was one of the Brighton directors. The referee said he had never heard such shouting and yelling across both directors' stands. We had five special players — we called them the Famous Five — playing for us at the time and it was the most exciting match I have ever been to. The score at the end was a draw — 4–4.

At that time, *Hugh and I* was the top television series in the country and when the Chester team were in London, I would always invite them along to the studios to watch the filming. It was strange — the players watching *me* for a change!

On another occasion, back in the Eighties, Terry ended

up supporting the opposition. I hadn't heard from him for ages but he suddenly rang me up at home. Chester were due to play a match at Aldershot in Surrey and Shân and I already intended to go. Although it wasn't actually Terry's team, it was close to where he lived and he had decided to go along and support them, especially as they were playing *my* team. He said to me on the phone, 'Are you going to see Chester play Aldershot?' When I said I was, he replied emphatically, 'I have never, ever, ever seen Aldershot lose at home.'

'OK, Terry,' I said cheerfully. 'We'll see.'

We got a nice welcome from the Aldershot and Chester directors when we arrived and made our way to our seats in the directors' stand, with Terry coming to sit with us. For most of the game Aldershot were ahead and Terry was going completely demented. He was screaming, shouting and jumping up and down, going bright red in the face, and even the Aldershot fans were beginning to look slightly embarrassed at this display. Despite Terry's exertions, Chester won 3–2. Yes, there was a God up there smiling down on us. Afterwards, we were invited for drinks in the board room, where Terry just sulked and sulked. He was just like a schoolboy who had had his catapult confiscated. He refused to have a drink or socialise, and when somebody said, 'Well, I expect you're glad for Hugh that his team won,' that was the last straw. He just sat in a corner and refused to talk to anybody. But that's just how he was. He hated losing ... especially to me!

Another great celebrity football fan is the lovely June

Whitfield who supports Wimbledon, where she lives. It was at a Wimbledon–Chester football match that Shân was to make one of her many football *faux pas*. She didn't really know anything about football until she met me — and she doesn't really know a lot more now! In fact, she gleefully tells the story when the legendary Alan Ball came into her office pub, the Stab, with one of the *Sunday Mirror* sports writers. They were chatting to Shân and the sports writer was called back to the office for a few minutes, leaving Shân with the footballer. Of course, she hadn't a clue who he was, having just about heard of Georgie Best at that time and that was only from reading about all his romances. So she gaily asked Alan Ball if he was a reporter or a photographer. He was not amused and didn't continue with the conversation after that.

Anyway, we went along to watch them play at Wimbledon. June was firmly ensconced with the Wimbledon directors and we were with the Chester directors, but we were able to manage friendly waves and mouthed greetings across the seats. Sitting in front of us was a young man in a tracksuit. About ten minutes after the game had started, he suddenly jumped out of his seat, ran to the front of the stand and started shouting and yelling at the players. Then he would come back to his seat for a few minutes ... and then jump up and do it all again. Shân was getting fed up with this. When he was in his seat, she started saying loudly, 'I didn't know they let loud-mouthed hooligans into the directors' stand.' And her comments went on and on throughout the match ... totally ignored, of course, by Mr Tracksuit Hooligan.

After the game — which we lost and several of our players were packed off on stretchers with various injuries (Wimbledon were not noted for being the gentlest of teams) — we were invited into the board room for drinks as usual. We were chatting to the Chairman of Wimbledon and some of the Chester directors when suddenly in walked Mr Tracksuit Hooligan, looking extremely cool and suave and very smart in an Yves St Laurent suit. To Shân's horror, he made his way straight over in our direction and, as he approached, the Chairman beamed and said, 'Oh, I don't think you've met our manager Dave Bassett, have you?'

Shân nearly sank through the floor with embarrassment. But Dave Bassett just shook her hand politely, smiled and said, 'No, we haven't met but I think you were sitting just behind me, weren't you?'

I don't think I've ever seen Shân with a redder face! Afterwards, she was furious. She kept demanding to know why he wasn't sitting in the dug-out as managers normally do. I couldn't answer that one, and couldn't help laughing when she kept wailing, 'Well, how was I to know he was the manager? He was sitting in the wrong place!'

Of course, we are always treated so well and greeted with such affection when we go to Chester that I am always happy to do any publicity for them, should they need it, in return. Several years ago, the Sealand Road ground was under threat of being sold and, there being no other suitable site, it would have meant that the city would have been without its own football club for the first time since the nineteenth century when it was first founded. The alternative — which did eventually come about — was for the players to share Macclesfield's ground, which was very unfair on the fans who would have to travel so far each week.

We had planned a quiet weekend in Chester around this time, just taking in a game and meeting up with old friends, but during the week I was contacted by the Liverpool *Daily Post* — which has a Chester edition — and asked my views on what was happening about the Chester ground. Feeling very strongly about it, I spoke frankly about what it would do to the morale of the city not having its own football club — and they published my comments. We arrived in Chester late on the Friday evening and, in the morning, were enjoying a leisurely breakfast in the hotel when I got a couple of phonecalls from newspapers asking if I was holding a press conference! Well, it was the first I'd heard of it. But then the club contacted me and said they thought I ought to meet the press there. They had been delighted by my comments in the *Daily Post* and wanted me to expand on them. So bang went the quiet weekend! Shân and I went off to Sealand Road to meet the press — they had me posing with my actor's face on with the ball in the goal and various other places. Then they asked me what my solution to the dilemma would be. I suggested that during the summer when the ground was not being used for football matches, perhaps they could stage Roman games which would be in keeping with the city's Roman heritage and attract many tourists and make a lot of money. Of course, I should have predicted the headlines before I spoke. They all ran along the lines of: COMEDIAN IN BEN HUR CHARIOT RACE BID. People must have thought I was mad!

However, one person who didn't was the Lord Mayor of Chester at the time who contacted me at the hotel and invited us for cocktails in the Mayor's Parlour that evening as he said he really wanted to meet me and thought my ideas were wonderful. I said I was very sorry but I couldn't make it as I was going to be at a football match that night — I think it was Tuesday by now and our stay had become rather extended! I told him, 'If you want to see me you'll have to come to the football ground.'

'Right then, I will,' he replied promptly.

And sure enough, straight after the game, he and his good lady were waiting for us in the Executive Bar. He was resplendent in his full regalia, having come straight from an official function. We enjoyed a few drinks and a good old chat together but sadly didn't really resolve the situation. In fact, the outcome was that Sealand Road *was* sold in the end and the team *did* go to Macclesfield for a time, but now we have a super new stadium — the Deva Stadium in Bumpers Lane — with a great club shop and very good facilities all round.

Originally, when the club was founded, the team had the nickname the Blues. Then when they went to Sealand Road, they became the Seals. But now they're at Deva Stadium they're the Blues again.

When I first took Shân to Chester, to the Sealand Road Stadium back in the very early Eighties before we were married, she was horrified. It was her first ever football match and, when we arrived, I was shown into the board room and she was herded into the Ladies Room. She found herself with a bunch of wives who she didn't know from Adam and who she said all seemed totally accepting of being segregated so that their husbands could all talk football without their wives interrupting. After the game, it was the same again, but they were sometimes invited into the board room after all the results had come up and had been discussed by the men. As you can imagine, when Shân finally came in with the other wives, they all sat quietly against the wall, but she stormed up to the Chairman and told him exactly what she thought of his archaic sexual discrimination — and she continued to wage this war every time she came to Chester. I agreed with her, but there was precious little I could do about it as the Board were all pretty old-fashioned. She carried on waging her campaign over several years, but they adhered to the policy — in fact, the Chairman used to hide when he saw her coming and eventually just gave up and let her in the board room whenever she wanted.

During this time, there was a story in the newspapers about Vicky Oyston, wife of the notorious millionaire OO Oyston, who was jailed for rape. Vicky, a former beauty queen, had become a director of Blackpool Football Club and, while visiting another club for a match, had been told she could not enter the board room because she was a woman — even though she was a director! Shân wrote sympathising with her and received a very nice letter back.

Around this time, we went to see Chester play at Fulham where Jimmy Hill was the Chairman. At half time, the Chester Chairman approached me and said Jimmy Hill would be delighted if I would join him and others for a drink in the board room — but Shân couldn't accompany me as women were barred. She was incensed as usual at the unfairness of it all, but told me to go and she would meet me in the other bar nearby. When she arrived there, the first person she saw was DJ 'Diddy' David Hamilton, an old mate of hers from her Fleet Street days and a keen Fulham supporter. He'd been invited to the board room, too, but had refused to go as he had his son and his girlfriend with him and the girlfriend was not allowed in.

We then heard not long after that match that Jimmy Hill was getting married again and Shân's first reaction was, 'I wonder if he'll bar his new wife from the board room, too.' And that suddenly struck a chord for a story. Using the 'new wife' angle, she got quotes from me, David Hamilton, Vicky Oyston and the MP Tom Pendry who was very much in favour of football becoming an inclusive family sport rather than a male preserve. It made a leading article in the *Daily Mirror* but I must say that the next time I went to Fulham, I was not invited into the board room — in fact, Jimmy Hill didn't even speak to me. I think someone had tipped him off that my wife was a journalist!

Things have changed drastically today and at Deva Stadium it's now mixed company both in the board room and the Executive Bar, although what some of those old-timers would have made of it, goodness only knows!

I also have some wonderful, fun-filled memories relating to my soccer love affair. Some years ago, before I met Shân, I was living in London and went along to see Chester play at Brentford in a Boxing Day match. Our great friend, actress Catherine Chase, came along with me. One of the Brentford directors was writer Willis Hall — who partners Keith Waterhouse — and he asked me if I would present some club prize or other on the pitch to the winner. I said I would be delighted. When I walked on to the pitch, a tremendous roar and tumultuous applause erupted from the crowd. My goodness! I thought. I didn't realise I was *that* famous! I must be more popular than I thought! And then I turned round ... and realised that the Brentford team had just run on to the pitch behind me!

On another occasion, I was well and truly put in my place at Chester when I had stayed behind in the board room for a few drinks with the directors. As we were a bit late leaving, we had to exit through the players' entrance where a few little boys were waiting with their autograph books for their football idols. As we passed them, suddenly one of the boys spotted me and said, ''Ere ... I've seen you on the telly!'

Another one echoed, 'Yeah ... I've seen 'im on the telly!'

I smiled benignly and reached out for their autograph books ... but they were promptly snatched away.

'Oh no,' said the little boy. 'We only have footballers.'

That really cut me down to size! So much for television stardom!

Although I am very much involved with the club, albeit mostly from a distance, I live too far away to become totally absorbed in it. Years ago, I was appearing in a show at Blackpool and the club chairman, a man called Reg Rowlands, came over to see me and asked me to be a director. Much as I would have loved to, I had to turn it down because I just would not have been able to attend enough matches to justify a say in the running of the place. But we do try and do our bit when we go up there by sponsoring a player or a ball for a match.

On one occasion, Shân and I sponsored a player called Roger Preece and paid for his football boots. Immediately after we had done that, we went to see a game and Roger scored *an own goal* with *our* boots! Shân, of course, wanted to know if we could get our money back!

As I said, we often also sponsor the ball for a match and usually I am asked to go out on to the pitch and present the ball to the Chester captain and have a photo taken for the next programme. On one occasion, we were spending ten days in Chester and attending two or three matches so we decided to sponsor the ball for two of the matches while we were up there. I presented the first ball, as usual, and when I said that I didn't really want to present the second one as well, they asked Shân to do it. Well, you'd have thought they'd asked her to present flowers to the Queen. She was so excited, but her only worry was walking across that vast pitch and falling flat on her face in front of everybody. She managed not to do that, and strode out apparently full of confidence with the steward, who passed her the ball as the two teams waited in the middle of the pitch. With a great beam she presented the ball, and the recipient leaned forward and whispered, 'Thank you. But I think you're supposed to give it to him.' And he pointed to the Chester captain! She'd only gone and given it to the captain of the opposition team!

'Well, they all look the same in shorts,' she said afterwards.

I'll do anything I feasibly can to help the club. For instance, a few years ago we were in dire financial straits and the fans — mainly the Independent Supporters Association, of which we are members and now have a place on the board — arranged a meeting at Westminster with the then Sports Minister Tony Banks. We decided it wasn't too far to go and we made our way up to the House of Commons to meet the Minister and plead with him to save our historic club.

As it turned out, it was bought by American football coach Terry Smith, backed by his father, Florida millionaire Gerald Smith. One of the reasons Terry said he had bought the club was because his family liked Chester Zoo, a patronising comment that did not augur well for the future. He seemed a likeable man but unfortunately he wanted to do everything — run the club, manage, coach, train — and unbelievably crossed swords with the loyal fans who are the heart and soul of the club. This culminated in him sacking manager Graham Barrow, much loved by the supporters because in previous years he had gained the club promotion to Division Two. When people ask who I support and then laugh derisively when I tell them, I have to remind them that not only did Chester produce Ian Rush and had Michael Owen's father playing for them, we also had Kevin Radcliffe, the former Everton and England skipper, as a manager and also Ken Roberts, who was very famous and now runs a sports training centre in North Wales. For better or for worse, I'm still very proud of the Blues and shall carry on supporting them whatever happens.

And something *has* happened. The club has been bought by Steve Vaughan, the Liverpool-based sports promoter, and we start another chapter. Chester City Football Club is alive — and kicking! And now, in 2002, the appointment of new manager Mark Wright of England and Liverpool looks like ensuring an exciting future. Long live the Blues! After all — as Bill Shankly famously said, 'Football isn't just a matter of life and death — it's far more important than that!'

14

Sussex-by-the-Sea

It was back in the early Eighties when I started to get itchy feet. We lived in a lovely big apartment in a large house in East Sheen in south-west London. It was very near the Sheen Gate of Richmond Park, not far from the Royal Ballet School and Princess Alexandra and Angus Ogilvy's home. We had lots of friends in the area, a great local pub and Shân's parents Jack and Margaret, with whom I got on very well, lived just around the corner. We were also not far from the BBC or from town, so I could always be up there quickly if necessary. So why did we want to move? I don't know. All I know is that I'd always dreamed of living by the sea. Perhaps it stemmed from my boyhood holidays in the little seaside resort of Llanfairfechan, or my day trips to Rhyl. It's daft really, I suppose, because I absolutely *hate* water! I just loathe the thought of being immersed in the sea and I don't particularly like washing my hair and feeling the water trickle all over my face and down my neck. But I do love looking at it or being on the sea in a boat!

Shân was all for the move as she loves the sea and is a keen, but not very strong, swimmer. Her star sign is Cancer (the crab) which gives her a love of water. Meanwhile, I'm Taurus (the bull) and can be very stubborn — although I must admit when it comes to some things, like DIY and electrical gadgets, I'm more like a bull in a china shop and run amok without knowing what on earth I'm doing. The trouble is that anything electrical, technical, or any type of gadget — they can all see me coming and break down! Having said that, I'm a dab hand at our three remote controls for the telly — well, I have to keep up to date with the football news, even out of season and, anyway, remote controls are apparently a 'man thing'.

Once the decision to move was made, we had to decide which area of coastline we would move to. Meanwhile, we had to sell our flat. We were quite sad about moving from such a lovely flat, although we were excited at the prospect of our new life. But as luck would have it, we managed to keep it in the family — Shân's parents lived in a large four-bedroom house five minutes from us. As Shân and her sister Lynne had both left home, they decided the house was far too big for them on their own and put it on the market while they looked around for a flat in the area. They looked at several, but could see nothing they liked ... except ours! So they bought it, solving a few headaches for us, and they still live there now.

We finally found our dream home in the tiny village of Rottingdean near Brighton. It was a chalet bungalow with a huge lounge and dining room and two bedrooms upstairs, and overlooked the playing fields of a private and very famous boys' prep school, which meant as long as the school existed the land would not be built on. The village also has a wonderful history of smuggling and boasts little alleyways with names like Whipping Post Lane. One house there was once the home of Captain Dunk, one of Rottingdean's most famous smugglers. The Library used to be a house called The Grange where the Black Prince, son of Edward III, is said to have stayed in the fourteenth century, and it is said that his ghost still haunts it and can be seen climbing along the roof of the building on dark, gusty nights.

The views were magnificent across to the Channel, the Sussex Downs and the lovely old windmill that stood on Beacon Hill. The black-and-white-timbered shops on the high street catered for just about everything, while the village pond on the green had lots of ducks and swans to watch and feed bread to. All our friends, of course, thought we were mad.

'You've been living in London so long,' they said (Shân is actually a Londoner born and bred), 'you'll go mad in some potty little village in the middle of nowhere. You'll be back in six months, we'll bet on it.'

But they lost their bet. Rottingdean had loads of super pubs and we soon made lots of new friends. Several people recognised me as soon as I walked through the door, and we soon became known in the local shops who would happily deliver anything you wanted at any time.

Shân and I have always found it easy to get on with new people, and I certainly think that's an advantage in my line of work! As I'm a pretty easy-going person, there are very few people I have come across that I actually dislike. But someone I didn't particularly take to was Dick Bentley, co-star of the famous radio show *Take It from Here*. In 1952, I did a Sunday concert in Weymouth in Dorset where I was the compère and Dick Bentley was one of the artistes. As the compère, I had to introduce all the acts. So I went round to Dick Bentley's dressing room that evening, while he had a few friends in. I knocked on the door and said, 'Good evening, Mr Bentley. I am the compère. Is there anything particular you would like me to say about you?'

Dick Bentley turned round, looked at me and retorted haughtily, 'If you don't know what to say about me, you shouldn't be the compère.'

That just about summed him up.

As with all dream places, there have to be a few snags, and we certainly had our share of them! The house — all the houses in the road were different — was originally designed by an architect for himself to live in. Consequently, there were plenty of little nooks and crannies and strange cupboards. We bought it from a rather elderly lady who had lived there nursing her ailing sister until she died, when the owner decided she needed a smaller bungalow in the village. It had been built just before the 1920s and I don't think much work had been done on it since then! There was a very large, uphill sloping back garden, where I think this lady spent most of her time, neglecting the actual bricks and mortar. The garden was incredibly well established and was a blaze of colour almost all year round. It had every type of herb you could think of from a very large rosemary bush to about 20 different varieties of mint, along with apple trees, a pear tree and an asparagus bed. There were hundreds of flowers and plants, too ... a lavender bush, huge poppies and daffodils in the front garden; rose bushes, tulips, blue, white and pink bluebells and peonies the size of footballs in the back garden. There were also a lot of weeds! Neither Shân nor I know anything about gardens, although she did once have an attempt at horticultural pursuits, wafting out into the back garden to pick some roses for the house! Feeling like the Queen of the countryside, she glided across the grass in a delicate pink summer dress, and promptly caught her skirt on a thorn causing a huge rip. And that was the end of her Charlie Dimmock aspirations! So we had a succession of 'little men' coming to mow the uphill lawn and see to the garden. Some were horticultural students who could only come for a few weeks in the holidays as they had to return to college, so we would have to start looking again for somebody else.

Meanwhile, the roof was in a terrible state, and the doorknobs kept falling off. At the time, I was doing a tremendous amount of theatre touring work, and Shân always came with me. Our neighbours were very good and said they would keep an eye on the place as we were away a great deal, but they were quite elderly and we couldn't expect them to go chasing burglars or doing too much! We felt quite embarrassed as there were quite a few housewives and retired people in the road who spent hours tending their gardens. Theirs were all immaculate, while we would return from a tour and consider opening ours to the public as a wildlife park!

We were away in Glasgow where I was doing a television play for BBC Scotland, when the hurricane in 1987 hit the Sussex coast. We'd put the television on early in the morning just to catch up on the news as I had to start filming at the crack of dawn. We couldn't understand why the newsreader was reading the news outside the studio but, of course, everything had gone down in the gales. And then the phone rang. It was our neighbour telling us that half our roof and the garden shed had gone ... and that, even worse, one of our friends in the village had died trying to pull down his garage door.

There was so much work to do, and so many workmen flitting back and forth for one thing and another, that the house was becoming a financial and personal millstone around our necks. And so we decided that as we were away so much, we really were flat people. We'd had ten really happy years in the village, but it was time to move on.

Amazingly, we sold the house, faults and all, quite quickly. The only trouble was that the buyers wanted to move in within the month and we had agreed to that, not wanting to lose the sale!

So where now? We didn't want to stay in the village and

walk past our old home every day and we didn't want to leave the Sussex coast either. A few years previously, I had done pantomime at the Connaught Theatre in Worthing, just a bit further west along the coast. We knew quite a few people from there, there was a good train service to London taking just over an hour, and so we settled on moving from East Sussex to West Sussex. We soon found a flat we liked, and decided to take it on for a year while we decided exactly where we'd like to live. We fancied North Wales or Cornwall, but they were both a bit far from London should we need to be there for work. And so ... that brings us up to date. We're still here! We've grown to love this seaside town with all its characters and its surrounding countryside. Every single window of our flat overlooks the sea, which makes my task of washing-up an absolute pleasure as I can just gaze out at the waves and the ocean with all its moods while I'm seeing to the pots and pans! To the amazement of most people, I actually *enjoy* doing the washing-up, especially after a Sunday roast when Shân has used just about every pan, bowl and plate in the place and the kitchen is a complete mess. I love to restore it to calm and actually find the whole process of washing-up very therapeutic. Sometimes Shân is asked, 'Have you got a dishwasher?'

She says, 'Yes,' and points at me!

The building itself has quite an amazing history, dating from Victorian times. We're not keen on modern blocks, but at least we don't have to see to the maintenance of this one — we just pay our service charges every quarter. It was built at the end of the nineteenth century, and is situated at the bottom of a sweeping, wide avenue that leads down to the seafront. The original idea was that it would be a very luxurious hotel. The flats were to be the rooms or luxury suites and the maisonettes on the ground floor were going to be shops. Across the road, a magnificent pier was planned.

At the top of the avenue — originally known as the Ladies' Mile — is a small railway station and the idea was that the 'nobs' of society would arrive by train from London, take a horse and trap down Ladies' Mile and then stay at the luxury hotel whilst relaxing on the pier. There was only one problem ... the pier was never built! In fact, the pier today is right down the other end of the promenade, nearly a mile away! Subsequently, the brilliant idea for the luxury hotel fell flat. And the building, which dominates the horizon like a bright, white wedding cake — became a bright white elephant. It remained empty for over 20 years until the 1920s when somebody had the idea to turn it into flats and maisonettes. And that's how it has remained ever since.

Of course, living in such an old building has its advantages ... and disadvantages. The rooms have lovely high ceilings and the thick walls are virtually soundproof, which is a great bonus. Mind you, the plumbing, which is ancient, can sometimes leave a bit to be desired but we do have plumbers who have been coming to the block for years and know the pipes back to front so they can usually sort out most problems.

There were quite a few jobs to be done when we moved in in April 1994. But they had to be put on the back burner for a while. It hadn't been easy moving from a house to a flat and the whole place was crammed with cardboard boxes — and that was after we'd had a house clearance! But the main trouble was that I had to go straight off touring in Ray Cooney's farce *Funny Money*; then to Abersoch to film with Tony Hopkins for *August*; and then on to do the theatre version of that in Mold, North Wales and Cardiff; and then straight into panto at Bromley in Kent where we were staying. So apart from the odd week or so at home, we didn't really start getting straight until about February 1995, almost a year after we'd moved in! Now I'm mainly doing just film and television work and cruising, we've got to know Worthing much better. Contrary to the common perception that it is a gloomy place — 'God's Waiting Room' — full of nursing homes, it is, in fact, a very lively up-and-coming town. There are plenty of colleges and foreign students, clubs and bars and every kind of restaurant you could think of. Apart from that, many top businesses are moving to Worthing, bringing lots of jobs to the area.

I must admit, though, that Worthing is probably one of the few places where it's safer to walk in the road! Some of the old ladies in their invalid cars think they are Stirling Moss and belt along the pavements, tooting their horns at anybody who dares get in their way! One old dear actually lost control and drove herself right through the window of the Salvation Army shop. Thankfully, she was fine ... which is more than could be said for the window! We have a marvellous modern shopping centre which people come from miles to visit, saying it is far better than nearby Brighton which has become very run-down these days.

There are always unusual street musicians to entertain you as you browse around and plenty of continental-style cafés to sit outside on the pavement in the warmer weather. When the sun shines in Worthing, you feel as though you could be on the Riviera! And leading down to the shops is a road that still has wonderfully unique family businesses — electrical and lighting shops where you can buy items that you would never find in today's chain stores.

A few years ago, we sold our car, Sophia, named after Sophia Loren because she was racing red. We intended to get another one at the time but we just haven't bothered. The reason for this is that we hardly used it when we moved here. Travelling to London is much simpler and quicker by train and, if I am doing a film or telly job, they will always send a car for me. Going into town in Worthing is simple, but it's difficult to park there if you take a car. We have a good little bus service which was dreadful when we first came here, I must say, but the company, Stagecoach, have received so much criticism in the press that they're doing their best to improve the service before they get lynched!

In the summer, we have the ideal form of transport to the shops — a little 'Thomas the Tank Engine'-style train runs right from the bottom of our road, along the seafront to the town centre. Sometimes, there are more local adults using it for their shopping than there are holidaymakers and children! And it's a wonderful way to travel to do the weekly shop. I really don't miss the car or driving at all. I find I get a lot more exercise and get out in the sea air more this way. I think it perhaps started a few years ago when Shân and I were driving to the Chichester Festival Theatre where I was appearing. Some idiot was going much too fast and cut us up on a roundabout, whereupon my dear wife, not famed for her tact and diplomacy, made a rude sign at him. This lunatic stopped right in front of us, still on the roundabout! He could have caused a pile-up. We were forced to pull over and he got out and ranted and raved. He went away eventually, but it was quite a frightening experience and I felt quite shaken up after it. You read more and more about road-rage these days and the more I read, the more I'm glad I'm away from these nutters.

However, if we do need to go anywhere, we have the perfect solution. We have an account with a local car firm called A & A. Some people might think this is an extravagance, but when you think about it we don't have to pay to tax a car, for servicing, MOTs, garage fees if anything goes wrong, petrol — and we don't have the worry of it being stolen or vandalised. We've actually had an account with A & A since we arrived in Worthing, and we think they really are the best car firm in the area. We know all the drivers well — and they know us — and they've become like a second family to us. When we arrive back from cruises, disembarking in the early morning and eager to get home, it's wonderful to see their friendly faces waiting for us on the dockside.

We've also made some good friends in this huge block, where sometimes you don't see people from one month to the next. It's certainly full of characters, from all walks of life. Some like us are owners and others rent, so some tenants might come and go without us even setting eyes on them.

One of our good friends is Anna Moore who lives a floor below us. Anna is a Reiki Master and a qualified aromatherapist and masseuse, so she is permanently charging about the place — to nursing homes, hospitals, private homes and treating people in her own home. Sometimes, Shân and Anna will go out for a walk on the beach at 6.00am before starting work and end up having tea and toast at a local café. Once, they were talking and laughing so much they didn't notice that the tide was coming in until they were up to their knees in water. They also, I think, hold the world championship record for shopping sprees!

Another good mate is our caretaker Brian Murray, who also practises Reiki. He's got a mad sense of humour and is forever playing tricks on us — although we generally get our own back.

A couple of years ago, the block was being re-painted — a marathon job which meant we had scaffolding up outside our windows for months. It drove us mad as we couldn't open the windows even in stifling heat, and we had no privacy unless we closed the curtains as the workmen were permanently on site. The noise was sometimes horrific and we began to feel very claustrophobic as though we were in some sort of prison. We knew it was all necessary, of course, but to get a bit of respite we took ourselves off to Swanage in Dorset for a week to get away from it all.

On our first day in Swanage, a bouquet of weeds arrived via Interflora, courtesy of Mr Murray, of course, in cahoots with Anna. The following morning, a parcel arrived in the post and was delivered to us at breakfast. It contained a piece of the scaffolding — just in case we were missing it!

While we were away, we were also having a new loo put in, which Brian was overseeing with the plumber. When we arrived back, our old loo seat was hanging from the front door, made up like a festive wreath with leaves, berries and nuts and a 'Welcome Home' message on it. We never know what we're going to find next!

Having said that, he really is a super caretaker and friend and he'll help anybody out. He's especially helpful to us with those horrendous DIY jobs that we're so useless at.

I've always thought that this stretch of the south coast should be called Showbiz-on-Sea, not Sussex-by-the-Sea. There must be as many entertainers — actors, singers, dancers, musicians — living down here as in London. Just around the corner from us, *EastEnders* star Tony Caunter, who plays car boss Roy Evans, has a home, and can often be seen in the local shops. And David Jason's brother, actor Arthur White, who regularly appears with him in *A Touch of Frost*, owns a hairdressing salon nearby. Not far away at Shoreham, Derek and Ellen Jameson rub shoulders with their neighbour, ex-*Heartbeat* and *Harbour Lights* star Nick Berry, along with astrologer June Penn, while just along from them are people like Frank Finlay, the indomitable Dora Bryan, Tony Adams (who plays Adam Chance in *Crossroads*), Mark Burgess, the former *Brookside* star ... and a host of other celebrities.

Fans don't really need addresses to write for autographs. I've had letters addressed to me which just say 'Hugh Lloyd,

Famous Actor, Somewhere in Sussex' — and they've arrived at our home! Our local postmen really are marvellous. So we really don't feel like moving again just yet ... if ever. Sometimes, we go on holiday to a place and say, 'Oh, I'd really like to live here.' But when all is said and done, I think we'd miss the sun streaming in the windows in the early morning, the sound of the waves rippling up the shingle — even the seagulls' early-morning alarm call even though they have no respect for the hour that they start!

If someone's feeling miserable for no particular reason, or one of our cruise audiences looks a bit subdued on a bright and beautiful day, I sometimes sing them a mad little ditty I penned many years ago, which could almost be a theme song for Victor Meldrew from *One Foot in the Grave*. It goes:

Start every day with a frown and a grumble
Just wake up each morning and curse
Folks always bank on a lucky tomorrow
Well tomorrow's today and today's a lot worse
Why should you smile every time that you stumble
Just use all the swears you love best
Start every day with a frown and a grumble
And get the damn thing off your chest!

I certainly don't wake up with a frown or a grumble these days. I sit at my desk looking out of the window, watching my wife walking along the prom to do the shopping, watching the sea, almost a turquoise blue in summer with the sunlight dancing like diamonds on the glittering water, and I think, What a lucky boy I am.

15

Life on the Ocean Wave

A couple of years ago, Shân and I decided to take a cruise together for the first time. As I have said, we both love the sea and are generally good sailors, so we were looking forward to lying about on the deck in the sunshine and sightseeing in exotic places. It was Shân's first experience of cruising, although I had done it several times before I met her and loved it.

Little did we know it was an experience which was to become a way of life for us — and change the way we live today. We decided on a Norwegian ship, the *Black Watch*, which is with the Fred Olsen line. The cruise was going to Lisbon, Agadir in Morocco and then on to all the Canary Islands, finally ending up in the beautiful flower island of Madeira. It was March but the weather forecast was pretty good for that part of the world.

We arrived in Lisbon in beautiful sunshine. We couldn't believe it was mid-March and spared a thought — though not for long — for those shivering at home! Then on to Agadir, where we were all told to stick very close to the tour guide for fear of being sold into white slavery or disappearing for ever in the maze of the mystical souk. After being treated to an amazing display by Arab horsemen and Moroccan snake charmers, we returned to the boat. Some had gone further afield to Marrakech and our sister ship, the *Black Prince*, was also in the area having docked at the famous Casablanca.

Over dinner, we were all chatting about our experiences that day when suddenly the Captain's voice solemnly announced in his strong Norwegian accent, 'Ladies and gentlemen, I am afraid to tell you there has been an outbreak of foot and mouth in Morocco today and through international shipping laws we may not be able to disembark in Gran Canaria tomorrow. There are forms to fill in in your cabins when you return.'

There was a stunned silence. If we couldn't disembark at the next port, who was going to let us in? Were we doomed to sail the Atlantic forever being shunned by everyone? Of course, then, as the British always do, we started to see the funny side of things — offering to go through the sheep dip. We couldn't honestly see how it affected us; after all, we'd hardly been out playing with the camels!

The forms were not what we expected at all. We thought they were going to be about our health, but they asked questions like, 'Have you bred any cattle in the last year?' One woman who lived with her son and daughter-in-law on a 'farm' which was no longer a working business, excluded the word from her address because she was terrified she would affect our clearance! We sailed on through the night, eventually docking at Gran Canaria alongside the *Black Prince*, whose passengers, if you'll excuse the pun, were all in the same boat, having visited Casablanca the previous day. It was a tense morning as we all hung over the deck rails waiting to see what was going on on the dock below. There had been no further announcements, so we hadn't a clue what was happening. The gangway was lowered and, all of a sudden, a procession of men with clip-boards came on board. Then a whisper went round. 'Fred Olsen's come on board!'

Now Fred Olsen is actually Fred Olsen Jr. He lives in Tenerife and apparently not only does he own the *Black Watch* and *Black Prince* — which bring a tremendous amount of tourist trade to the islanders — but he also owns all the ferries that run between the Canary Islands. What he said to the men with clip-boards we will never know, but within ten minutes of him stepping on board we had clearance to go ashore.

At this point, I feel I must mention our Captain — Captain Thor. I'm afraid I must say that all the men hated him and all the women — including Shân — were madly in love with him! He was the classic tall, blond Norwegian who listed his hobbies as riding his Harley Davidson around the fjords! Our cabin seemed to be part-way along the access route from the bridge, and very often Shân would open the door to find him outside. She would then promptly swoon and, after a quick chat with him, fall back into the cabin again. She became the envy of every woman on the boat who, every dinner time, would ask her eagerly, 'Have you found him outside the cabin today?' The men just used to go out on deck, watch him manoeuvre into a dock and mutter, 'Call himself a Captain!' It was all in good fun, though, and as Shân pointed out, every female ought to fall in love with the Captain for a short while!

We made some good friends on that trip. We got chatting to a couple — Graham and Terry Baker — who, it transpired, lived not far from us in Lewes. One evening, Shân was having a drink with Terry and said to her, 'Some of these people are going on about doing five cruises a year! I wonder where on earth the money comes from.'

Terry smiled. 'They might have won the lottery,' she ventured.

There was something about the look on her face that made Shân question her further. 'Are you trying to tell me something?' she said.

And yes, it transpired that Graham and Terry had won £1.3 million on the lottery and it hadn't changed them a bit! In fact, the first thing Terry had said was, 'I don't have to move, do I?' They've since become good mates of ours and we meet up from time to time, either at their place or ours.

Having had a wonderful time in the Canary Islands — where I was delighted to find a Spar where I could buy a litre of vodka for about £2.99 — we moved on to Madeira.

What a beautiful island, full of sunshine and flowers. We decided to take out a second mortgage and have a drink at the famous Reid's Hotel from where we could see the entire bay and watch our ship in dock. It was breathtaking — but you wouldn't want to pay for more than one gin and tonic! We took a taxi back to the ship and commented on the beautifully warm weather. The taxi driver shook his head. He'd just dropped a fare up in the mountainous region where apparently it was absolutely freezing! So we returned to the ship, and I must say at this point that throughout the whole voyage I had been recognised and talked to by just about the whole ship. I'd signed autographs, posed for photos and been kissed by strange ladies. Not that I minded, of course — after all, it's an occupational hazard. But it was at this point on the way back home that the cruise director Michael Burke approached me. 'Look,' he said, 'why on earth are you paying for this cruise? You'd only have to do a couple of talks and you could do it for nothing.'

Shân and I looked at each other. The idea had never even entered our heads. But we decided we loved cruising. We could see the world for free — so why not? And so *An Audience with Shân and Hugh Lloyd* was born. We decided to do a double act, with Shân interviewing me about my life in showbusiness, starting off with the Hancock days, then another talk about Terry Scott and *Hugh and I*, and finally ending up with Hugh and Hopkins, talking about my work on *August*. These talks, of course, are all interspersed with a few gags, silly songs and a bit of domestic banter between us which the audience love. However, between the time of leaving the *Black Watch* and having sorted this out, we decided to take another 'paid for' cruise later that year. This was really because it was going to the Holy Land which I had always longed to see. This time it was on a much larger ship — P&O's *Arcadia* — and, after that experience, give me a small liner any time. The cruise was in August, a mistake for anyone who wants to enjoy a leisurely cruise, as the schools were on holiday. Don't get me wrong, I love children — why would I have done so many pantos otherwise? But a cruise liner is just not the place for them. Once they've got fed up with the pool and explored every deck, they get bored and, of course, they're trapped, so they start doing silly things and become a danger to themselves and to everybody else. And that's exactly what happened on this cruise. As various children had started to become a bit restless and unruly, there were countless tannoys from a very stern-sounding Captain saying, 'I am responsible for this ship. Parents are responsible for their children.'

Now it just happened that the Chairman of P&O, Lord Sterling, was on board having a holiday, so the entire crew were walking on eggshells. Having a horde of rampaging kids on board did not help and they were doing everything they could to alleviate the situation. Things finally came to a head with two major events.

One night, a gang of youngsters — presumably their parents were in the bar — got out of their cabins, went up to the Conservatory where the breakfast buffet is served and, for some unknown reason, smashed every plate they could find.

Then another tearaway was rushing down a corridor, banged straight into Lord Sterling and head-butted him in the groin! That was it. One family were turned off the boat when we finally docked at Haifa, gateway to the Holy Land.

We were really excited about this particular trip. It was going to be a long coach journey to Jerusalem and Bethlehem in a blistering 100°F, but we were all prepared to put up with it. And what a disappointment. If anybody really feels they could derive any sense of awe at being in the Garden of Gethsemane and at the Wailing Wall, it was taken away by the commercialism and the hordes of coaches and tourists — of whom I must admit we were a part. And so on to Bethlehem where we made a stop at the Holy Manger store! What an emporium of tackiness. You almost expected to find blow-up Virgin Marys — it wasn't that far off it. Shân asked, tongue-in-cheek, if they sold shepherds or Wise Men you could float in the bath. The shop assistant was most concerned and said no, but did she think there would be a market for them? So who knows? They may well have a new line by now!

Sitting outside the store in the sunshine was an old man who looked as though he had stepped straight out of the pages of the Bible. Shân was fascinated and went to take a photograph of him, but he shook his head sternly. Suddenly, a young man from the store appeared and said something to him, took the camera from Shân and motioned her to go and sit on his lap! This was a bit too much but she did get her treasured picture taken with Methuselah, even though he didn't seem too happy about it. When we finally reached the tiny Bethlehem High Street crammed with coaches, cement mixers — they'd just apparently realised that the millennium was approaching — and various other vehicles, we discovered that our rather inept coach driver had parked miles away from the actual Holy Manger site. He'd done the same thing twice in Jerusalem. In the scorching heat, we decided not to venture up there just to see a hole in the wall, but to wait in the high street. Shân wanted to cross the road to a shop she had seen but hadn't a clue how she was going to make it across the busy street. Hovering on the kerb, she suddenly found herself taken by the hand by a very handsome young tourist policeman who stopped the traffic and accompanied her safely across. He did the same for her return — and I'll swear she crossed that road eight times!

It was a memorable trip but, as I said, I think smaller boats suit us much more. There, you are a person. On a huge ship you feel rather like a number — it's just the same with a family-run hotel or a huge chain.

On our return home, pretty exhausted and needing a holiday to get over our holiday, we suddenly got a phone call from an agent. He said he represented guest speakers on liners, had been given our names and would we be available to do talks on Cunard's *Saga Rose* in a couple of weeks' time? Well, we couldn't say no, could we? Not if we were going to launch this new free cruising lifestyle of ours! So, of course, we agreed and, having unpacked, found ourselves whizzing round to the dry-cleaners again getting ready for yet another bout of packing.

The *Saga Rose* is quite an old ship which has been tarted

up and refurbished to make it a very desirable cruise liner. Our fellow guest speaker on this trip was Carol Cleveland from the Monty Python team who was doing her first talk and was as nervous as we were. The talks seemed to go down pretty well, but ours needs a sort of intimate area where you feel you are just having a chat with the audience instead of lecturing them and the room we were in was vast so we felt at a bit of a disadvantage. Obviously, you are expected in these talks to 'keep it clean' and not tell any stories that are too risqué — not that we had any anyway — as you have such a mixed audience. However, the rather flamboyant ship's doctor, who had served in the Falklands amongst other places, decided that he was going to give talks, too. And with his there were no holds barred! He could tell the most outrageous stories and get away with it, being the ship's doctor. It was hard to compete with that!

We did get to see some lovely places, including Florence — where Shân insisted on having some genuine Italian spaghetti bolognese which must have been the worst we've ever tasted — and Rome. I went to Rome on my own as it involved a long coach trip which Shân hates, and she'd had enough of them by then. We travelled for a long time in silence, our guide saying absolutely nothing. Eventually, we reached the outskirts of the city, with its most famous churches and buildings coming into view. And then the guide stood up. 'On the right,' she said, 'we have the Methodist Church.'

Methodist Church! All this history, and all she could point out was the Methodist Church. I couldn't stop laughing. However, I did get to sit on a hill, eat an Italian ice cream and watch a Punch and Judy show, so all in all I was quite happy!

Shân, meanwhile, had managed to find herself a magazine article in the shape of one of the lady passengers who made unusual hats and owned a shop called 'Over the Top'. This lady used to hold Mad Hatter tea parties on the pavement outside her shop and made hats for Ascot and such events. So it was quite a profitable venture as it turned out.

Our next booking came at very short notice. We got a phonecall from the agent on a Thursday asking if we'd do a cruise to the Land of the Midnight Sun. I'd never been to Norway and had always wanted to see the fjords, so I said yes almost immediately.

'There's just one snag,' he said. 'It's a bit short notice.'

'How short?' I replied.

'You sail on Tuesday.'

Anybody who has ever cruised will know it usually takes a lot longer than four or five days to get ready for it, but Shân and I were beginning to feel like real seasoned cruisers by then, so we agreed. The ship we were to sail on from Harwich was the *Ocean Majesty*, a Greek vessel which is frequently chartered by Page and Moy, the travel agents. We arrived at the docks with no boarding passes or tickets as there hadn't been time to send them. There was a bit of negotiation with security but all was resolved quite quickly and we were allowed on board, thank goodness!

The first person we were to meet was a lady for whom we now feel a tremendous amount of respect, admiration and affection — the cruise director Christine Butler. Christine's late husband Dave was one of the Comedians and also worked the cruise ships with her, but a few years ago he died very suddenly and Christine has carried on working relentlessly all hours for the sake of his memory. Alongside her as her deputy she also has her lovely daughter Danielle, whose boyfriend Mark, as well as being the ship's DJ, acted as the technician and lighting man for our talks. He was absolutely wonderful and we always felt as safe as houses doing the chats when Mark was in attendance — he was always solid as a rock. Also on this trip was an old pal, ventriloquist John Bouchier. John told us that he often has trouble coming through airports with his dolls because the heads are detached and when they go through the X-ray machine it looks as though he's a mass murderer carrying around the severed heads of his victims!

'What happens when you explain?' we asked him.

'I usually have to give them a show before they let me go,' he sighed.

Another of the acts was singer Bobby Reid who lives near us in Bognor Regis and who we were to meet up with again on another cruise. We found the *Ocean Majesty* an exceptionally friendly ship. It was a real team and nobody could do too much to help each other. The only problem really was that the Greeks wanted things done one way and Page and Moy — who were really in charge — wanted them done another. The Captain, we gather, could be pretty argumentative and I think Christine had more than her fair share of attempts to negotiate with him.

He did have quite a sense of humour, though. One day we went ashore by tender and, on returning in the lifeboat, the Captain was also a passenger. As we went to get off and get back on board I motioned to the Captain to go first. He shook his head. 'Oh no, Captain always last to leave ship,' he grinned.

Talking of lifeboats, we had a lovely large cabin on Diamond Deck with a picture window. The only problem was that there was a lifeboat hanging right outside it! If you peered under it, you could just about see the ocean rolling past, but we had a laugh about it and used to say that at least if there was an emergency we could just smash the picture window and be first in our own lifeboat!

Our talks went down exceptionally well on the *Ocean Majesty* — perhaps because it was such an intimate, friendly boat. The theatre we performed in was small by comparison to others, but it suited us perfectly. On this boat, though, we had to give each talk twice — which we didn't mind at all — because you could only fit half the passengers in at one time. So we used to do 45 minutes, have a short break, and then do it all over again for the next audience. We were a bit startled at first when Christine put us on at 9.30 in the morning. We didn't think anybody would turn up at that hour. How wrong we were. We were packed out and the audiences are at their best at that time. They're up and about early in the sunshine, having had their breakfast and strolled the deck and are eager to be entertained. If you do the talks in the afternoon, then people have had their lunch and are liable to fall asleep! In fact, I often announce a change in the programme at the beginning of our talk. I say, 'At 3.15, there will be a Staying Awake contest in the Lido Lounge!' It always gets a good laugh, anyway.

Shân also acquired herself an extra job on this trip — as a pencil monitor! The pianist in the main lounge was a wonderful character, a Yorkshireman called Jeff Shaw, and he also used to run the various quizzes that go on throughout the day. We always enjoyed doing these for a bit of fun and, on one occasion, Shân offered to help Jeff take the pencils and paper round to the passengers taking part. This soon became a full-time job, but Jeff used to complain jokingly that Shân took about an hour to get round the room as she stopped to have a chat with every single table!

The trip up the fjords presented us with the most spectacular scenery I think I have ever witnessed. It's as though God started the world from here with a big explosion. There are literally hundreds of islands, some the home for just one or two houses, scattered around the ocean. We used to say, 'You'd have to get on with the neighbours!' Huge fjords with picturesque waterfalls pouring down them, and again maybe one house perched on the top. How did it get there — and why?

Of course, the cruises only run in the summer when they have their constant hours of daylight. The rest of the year they're in darkness. We were warned not to have a drink ashore because the prices are phenomenal. That's because there's such a high rate of alcoholism in Norway. It's not surprising, really, being stuck in all that darkness all year round, there's nothing much else to do, I suppose. We gather there are a number of illicit stills in Norwegian homes and, in fact, one of the guide books warned us that if we were invited to a Norwegian's home and offered a drink to be very careful — what we were drinking could be akin to aircraft fuel!

We sailed on, making a couple of stops at places with unpronouncable names and eventually arrived at the little town of Geiranger, which is set in a fjord. The sun was shining, the place was as pretty as a picture and it was just what we'd always imagined Norway to be. We were anchored just off the coast, as was a large American boat on which we heard the passengers had paid something like £1,000 a night to have their every whim pandered to. We went ashore as usual in our little lifeboats, while they had power launches. And on shore they had an awning with white-gloved waiters serving them champagne as they landed.

Back on board, we all hung over the deck rails, feeding the seagulls bread rolls and watching the comings and goings of the wealthy Americans, making fairly derisory comments, I must admit, as we went along. We really did feel like the poor relations! We got our moment of glory, though, when in the calm, still sunshine, a sudden strong gust of wind blew the awning down right on top of the white-gloved waiters and their passengers.

The highlight of the cruise — which happened to be on Shân's birthday — was a trip to the North Cape — the northernmost point — to the Land of the Midnight Sun. It was to be quite a long coach trip from the dock at

Honningsvag. This little port has one shop featuring a large troll and a reindeer outside, and a club — which must be about the only form of social life the residents ever get to see. We set off across the most spectacular countryside. Reindeer grazed contentedly alongside the road and we were told we would soon be arriving at a traditional Sami camp. The Sami were a nomadic people who herded the reindeer from place to place in days gone by. We arrived at the small reconstructed Sami encampment to see that it was opposite a house with a satellite dish and Range Rovers parked in the driveway. We had this vision of them watching out for the coaches, throwing on their traditional costumes and rushing across the road, because I'm sure they're pretty modernised by now! They had a type of wigwam showing how things were done in the past and a Sami — who looked as though he was wearing a pantomime finale walk-down costume — was holding on to a rather moth-eaten-looking reindeer. I was quite surprised at how small the reindeer were — I'd expected them to be much larger somehow. Anyway, I was taking in all the culture and history of the indigenous population, when suddenly Shân came rushing up in great excitement. 'They take credit cards in the shop!' she exclaimed. All this history, and that's all she could think of!

Leaving the Samis, we headed off towards the North Cape. Unfortunately, it was very misty when we got there so we didn't get the full benefit of what we'd come to see, but it was still an experience feeling that you were on top of the world. Eventually, we headed back for the boat where Shân rounded off her birthday by being serenaded at dinner with half-a-dozen waiters singing 'Happy Birthday' to her and presenting her with a cake. She says it was certainly a birthday she'll never forget!

There was also a day of whale-watching. We were in an area where whales were supposed to appear and many passengers spent hours hanging over the rails watching in vain for these great beasts. However, not a single whale appeared, and on the last night when we were all singing 'Whale Meat Again', Christine suddenly appeared with an enormous inflatable plastic whale which she thought might be a consolation for those who had been desperate to see one. Of course, there are always plenty of dolphins and the like to see, but usually by the time it's been announced that there's a school of dolphins alongside one particular part of the ship, everybody rushes to see them and by the time they get there, they're gone!

We had quite a calm journey back across the North Sea, which was in complete contrast to the conditions on our way out to Norway. On the second night of the cruise, it had been terribly choppy and about 80 per cent of the passengers were missing at dinner. But as I said, Shân and I tend to be good sailors, so we were OK. The only irritating thing was getting from A to B with the ship lurching all over the place. You had to plan your route from the bar to the toilets meticulously, working out what you could hang on to on the way.

We were delighted to be asked back on the *Ocean Majesty* within the year, this time for a nine-day

Mediterranean cruise. The only snag as far as we were concerned was that we had to fly to Naples to join the ship. Now it's not the actual flying that concerns me, I just hate all the hassle at the airports. I don't mind flying if it's for work and somebody else is paying, but I would *never* use it as a form of transport when going on holiday. I'd take the ferry, train, hovercraft, donkey ... anything but get on a plane in those circumstances! And I think our experience at getting to Naples illustrates why I feel this way.

We were glad to learn we only had to fly one way and would be returning on the *Ocean Majesty* to Harwich. Our flight was at around 6.00am from Gatwick — which, of course, is not far from us and we were due to arrive at the airport for check-in around 4.00am. Our lovely caretaker Brian came and gave us a knock at around 3.30am to make sure we were up and about and the taxi arrived shortly afterwards.

At that time of the morning, we were sure that check-in would be easy. Hardly anybody about, we'd be straight through in no time and might even have breakfast in the departure lounge ... or so we thought. Which probably goes to show that we haven't flown anywhere for ages. It was bedlam! Hundreds of people and their luggage milling about everywhere. We couldn't understand it — until we learned that the check-in conveyor belts had broken down. Shân was already fed up, having scrupulously weighed all our luggage on the bathroom scales. When you arrive at a port there's no limit to what you can take. The luggage is swept away by a porter the moment you arrive and the next time you see it it's in your cabin. But this was a Page and Moy charter flight with all the passengers heading for the *Ocean Majesty* so there was nothing we could do about it. We had to wait an hour-and-a-half before we could even check in. There was nowhere to sit and you could hardly move for the crowds. Eventually, having checked in there was no time to browse around the shops in the departure area or purchase any tax-free goods. We were all herded — after a two-mile journey on the travelator, I felt like a piece of luggage on a conveyor belt myself — into a room prior to boarding. And there were more delays to come. About 20 minutes after we should have taken off, there was an announcement from the pilot. Sorry about the delay, he said, but they were waiting for some books to be brought on board.

Another 20 minutes or so passed, and another announcement. The books had turned up but they'd brought the wrong ones so someone had gone off to get the correct ones. 'It's probably a book on how to fly a plane,' muttered one irate passenger.

Eventually, an hour late, we took off for Naples. After about half-an-hour everybody started to feel terribly cold. Coats that had been thrown into the overhead lockers were all coming down as we sat and shivered, trying to warm up with hot tea — or cold whisky in some cases, I noticed! We asked the stewardess why it was so cold.

'Oh,' she said. 'Some people at the back said they felt too hot so we turned the heating off.'

'Well turn it back on!' cried the majority of the plane. So they did and things were a lot more comfortable after that.

It was a relief after our ordeal to touch down at Naples Airport in brilliant sunshine. Page and Moy coaches were due to meet us all but we had to retrieve our luggage from what seemed a highly complicated double carousel. Stupidly, we had done nothing to distinguish our plain black suitcases and Shân was going demented trying to find them. Then, suddenly, we heard a voice.

'Hello, I saw your names on the list and thought I'd come down to meet you.' It was Jeff Shaw, the pianist from the boat, with whom we had got on so well before. Seeing a familiar face was like a haven in a storm and we threw our arms around him gratefully. We were soon on board ship which was docked in a very industrial part of Naples. Many of the passengers had been travelling by coach all night to get to the airport so not many people felt like going ashore. So we just lazed in the unfamiliar sunshine on the deck, sipping drinks and falling asleep from time to time, the shadow of that great volcano Mount Vesuvius looming ominously over us. Shân tried to video the volcano as we steamed out of port that evening, but she couldn't find it! 'How can you lose Mount Vesuvius, for goodness sake?' she kept wailing.

It had been a great surprise reunion with many familiar faces when we got on board. Apart from the lovely Christine Butler and her family and all the Page and Moy staff, we discovered that the comedian was a chap called Bobby Dazzler — we had met him on our very first cruise on the *Black Watch*! The singer Bobby Reid was also on board and, to my great astonishment, a wonderful lady trumpeter called

Joan Hinde. I hadn't seen Joan since the Fifties when we had worked together in some show or other entertaining the troops. It transpired that she and her husband Ken, like Bobby Reid, also live in Bognor Regis, so we were all close neighbours.

Joan is an extraordinary lady ... and can she blow that trumpet! She's also got a great sense of humour. She told us that she's often been likened in appearance to the former speaker and Tiller girl Betty Boothroyd. Apparently, she was told by a member of one of her audiences that a lady had commented to her neighbour, 'Doesn't she look like Betty Boothroyd?'

'I don't know, love,' came the reply. 'I never watch *Coronation Street*.'

On another occasion, Joan had been playing a theatre somewhere and when she came to leave from the Stage Door it was pouring with rain. Her husband Ken was with her and he told her, 'You wait here, love, and I'll go and get the car from the car park and bring it round.' Agreeing gratefully, Joan asked him if he would take her stage dress and trumpet and put them in the car. As he walked across the car park in the teeming downpour, frock over one arm and trumpet in the other hand, he heard someone say loudly, 'You see, I *told* you that trumpet player was a man!'

We met really pleasant new company as well at our dinner table that night in the form of the classical guitarist Martin Vishnik who had brought his brother-in-law Mark along as his guest. Both were very keen walkers and climbers and Mark had a bit of a hair-raising experience later on in the cruise when we docked at Gibraltar. Mark — whom we non-climbers decided was quite mad — thought he would climb up the Rock. He got to the top and was making his way down some steps on the way back, which had no railing. As he picked his way carefully down them, a Barbary Ape suddenly leapt out from a little cove it had been hiding in. It gave him such a fright he nearly fell over the sheer edge into oblivion.

After Naples, our next port of call was to be the picturesque French island of Corsica, birthplace of Napoleon Bonaparte. We used quite an unusual mode of transport to see round this compact island in the form of a little 'toy-town' train that took us to all the sights, including Napoleon's statue, and ended up back in the centre of town. Quite a lot of places have these little trains and we often use them when we can, whenever there's time, as they're a really enjoyable way to travel and see everything at the same time. The only problem can be that sometimes they have taped commentaries and, if there's a traffic hold-up or the driver goes a bit too fast, then they're hopelessly out of synch and you find yourself looking for buildings you passed ages ago and didn't know what they were! Unfortunately, when the ride ended Shân spotted a little man covered in balloons and dressed in a funny costume in the square. She made the mistake of pointing at him ... of course, he gleefully bounded over and I just couldn't get rid of him until I'd parted with a few well-earned francs! She's always had a thing about balloons!

After Corsica, the next stop was Nice on the glorious

Cote d'Azur. We docked just outside the town centre alongside some enormously expensive-looking yachts, and spent some time drooling over them before we finally disembarked. Nice was bathed in beautiful sunshine and, after sitting on the main Promenade des Anglaises for a while, we got up to take a stroll. We were immediately accosted by a gentleman — if you could call him that — from the Ivory Coast who was about 7ft tall. I remembered then that they were all over the place the last time I was here, pestering people on the beaches with their mock ivory jewellery and such like. He seemed pleasant enough to start with and told us, 'My parents live in Manchester, my sister lives in Ireland, my brother lives in Scotland and my other sister lives in Wales and I support Manchester United.' Well, he certainly had every part of the British Isles covered for any would-be customer who was stupid enough to believe him. We couldn't get rid of him. He dogged our every footstep along the prom, trying to foist 'gold' rings on us. I kept telling him we had no money and that we'd left it all on the boat but he still wouldn't go away. And then he started to get angry. It was quite frightening really — I thought we were going to be mugged. Finally, he said threateningly to me, 'You don't like black men.'

Then I really saw red. I drew myself up to my full height — which was just about to his waist — and replied, 'There are two kinds of people as far as I'm concerned — good people and bad people.' And I glared at him.

He had no answer to that. Knowing he ranked in the second category, he just turned and slunk away, tail between his legs. And that was the last we saw of him. So we just carried on soaking up the sunshine and sipping cocktails until it was time to return to the *Ocean Majesty*.

The following day's port of call was Barcelona. It was a Sunday and, much to Shân's annoyance and my delight, we were informed that most of the shops would be shut. It was only a short walk into the town but along the pavements they have the most ridiculous sloping cement blocks, the same colour as the paving stones, and Shân nearly went flying over one. I just managed to pull her out of the way in time. We really couldn't see the purpose of them. Somebody said they were to stop cars parking on the edge of the pavements, but why on earth they couldn't have been of a contrasting colour so that people could see them I don't know. Inevitably, somebody was going to come a cropper and, unfortunately, the victim was Joan Hinde. We met up with her later in the main street. She was terribly shaken up. She'd fallen flat on her face over one of these wretched things and was terrified that she had cracked her jaw — a bad enough injury for anybody, but even worse for a trumpeter. After the fall, she'd gone back to the ship to see the doctor who assured her that nothing was broken — she was only bruised. And then Ken had made her come straight back out again before she lost her nerve. But the unfortunate episode really left her shaken up for the rest of the cruise.

Contrary to the information we'd been given about the shops being shut, Barcelona was alive and buzzing on a Sunday. There was a lively street market selling jewellery, paintings and all sorts of crafts, all the bars and restaurants were open, street musicians and stilt walkers abounded and several of the shops — where Shân insisted on buying an extremely large blue sombrero — were open. So never believe what you read in the guide books!

After a refreshing jug of *sangria* at a local restaurant, where we met some people from my home town, Chester, we headed back, ready to sail for our next port — the fun-loving, notorious island of Ibiza.

We docked there — right in the centre of the town — in the early morning and made our way ashore at around 9.30am. It was like a ghost town — virtually everything was closed. They'd obviously been partying all through Sunday night! There was a small tobacconist and postcard shop open so we went in there. The proprietor asked us if we were from the boat and what time we were sailing. When we told him it was only a short stay — we had to be back on board just after noon — he gabbled something in Spanish to a woman standing by him. Within ten minutes, every single shop was open and a market had been set up. How they could have missed seeing an enormous ship dock in their tiny town centre a couple of hours previously I do not know!

Ibiza is a maze of narrow streets and alleyways, littered with shops and bars and clubs. It really is a shopper's paradise — I had trouble getting Shân back on the boat — with really good bargains of all sorts — clothes, jewellery and shoes. And, of course, it was out of season for lager-lout time — I certainly wouldn't want to go back there then.

Gibraltar was the next stop, a place we have visited several times. This is always our duty-free pick-up point as everything is so cheap. The winding high street is always packed with bargain-hunters, many of them heading for Marks & Spencers; why, I don't know, as it is the one place where the prices don't seem very different to home. We had a drink in the Rock Hotel slightly further out. The views from there are magnificent across the bay, but as neither Shân nor I are very keen on heights, we've never bothered to take the cable car up the Rock to see the Barbary Apes. On a previous visit to Gibraltar, we saw for the first time one of those 'life statue' artistes who moves when you throw money into his bucket. This one was painted white from head to foot and looked quite phantom-like. Having not come across one before, Shân, delighted at this apparition, got the camera out — not realising you had to put money in the tin in order to take a photo. She snapped away — and suddenly this 'statue' came to life and waved his fist at her! 'I'm not giving him any money if that's his attitude,' said Shân indignantly, only then realising that's what she should have done before taking the photo. So she just snapped away gaily — until the statue snapped, and started chasing us down the street! We managed, fortunately, to get lost in the crowds and hide at the back of a bar but I don't think she'll be taking many more pictures of 'live' statues in future!

Leaving Gibraltar, we were watching the pilot boat guiding us out when, to our astonishment, we saw on the side of it that it came from the Mumbles. That's a resort on the Gower Coast in South Wales where Shân's sister Lynne lives ... so what it was doing in Gibraltar, we don't know!

Lisbon was our final port of call and it was here we hit

bad weather for the first time in the cruise. It was grey, overcast and drizzly and we couldn't summon up much more enthusiasm than to wander into the city centre, have a glass of their famous local 'green' wine which is absolutely delicious and do a bit of shopping.

It was to be 'red, white and blue' night on board that evening. I always have the perfect costume for it — no Union Jack Hats or waistcoasts for me. As I've mentioned before, I hate dressing up and am always the first with the bow-tie off on formal nights, but for this particular evening I wear a white T-shirt, blue trousers ... and colour my nose with a bright red lipstick! Well, everybody expects actors to be slightly mad!

And speaking of madness, I was appearing in Lyme Regis in Dorset with a famous comic of the day, Harold Berens, who was the star of the hit radio show *Ignorance Is Bliss*. Harold — whose catchphrase was 'What a geezer!' — and I went over to Weymouth one day to meet 'Monsewer' Eddie Gray, who was the seventh member of the Crazy Gang. He really was a fore-runner to Tommy Cooper as he was a mad comedy juggler with a great deadpan act. When we went to meet him, for some reason we were invited to tea with the Lady Mayoress. When we got there and were handed our tea and cakes, everything Eddie Gray said would be repeated two minutes later by Harold Berens. For instance, Eddie would say, 'It's really hot today. We had a terrible journey over.' And two minutes later Harold would say, 'It's really hot today. We had a terrible journey over.' They carried this on throughout the afternoon. Of course, they were playing a joke. I was in absolute stitches and trying not to let the Lady Mayoress see me laughing. But I think the poor lady was too mystified to notice. She was totally embarrassed and baffled. But then, what do you expect from a member of the Crazy Gang?

It's always nice to get home after a cruise, however much you've enjoyed it. You need to relax a bit before facing the unpacking, when you discover things you'd forgotten you'd bought along the way! But there wasn't to be much relaxation for us after this cruise. A couple of weeks later, we were off again, this time on the *Black Watch*, back up the Norwegian fjords. It was rather nostalgic boarding the *Black Watch* at Dover as we had not seen her since we did that very first cruise together — as passengers. Now here we were, back again, but working! We were looking forward to seeing some familiar faces, especially among the wonderful Philippino crew. They work so hard and can't do enough for you. It's really sad, in a way, because many of the waiters are medical or law graduates but, of course, there's no work in their own country and this is the only way they can send money home to support their families. They work for around nine months a year and many of them have young children so they miss seeing them grow up. But they seem to accept cheerfully that this is how life is for them — and generally they're always smiling and laughing. Our cabin attendant, however, was a little Thai girl with the unbelievable name of ... Porn! She knew what her name meant in English and thought it terribly funny. Our waiter, a Philippino, was called Dan and, although he only spoke a little English, his favourite phrase for everything was 'lovely jubbly'!

We set sail again across the North Sea and our first port of call was to be Lerwick in the Shetland Islands. We arrived on a grey, gloomy day and I must admit the Shetlands looked exactly as I'd imagined them! We anchored off Lerwick and boarded the tenders to go ashore. Someone had said that the town centre was about two miles away but there was a shuttle bus service in operation. However, when we landed there was no sign of a shuttle bus ... just a fleet of taxis circled around the dockside. I asked one of them if he could take us to the town centre. 'Well, I would,' he said. 'But you're in it.' And that just about summed up Lerwick! A straggle of rather nondescript shops selling Shetland hats and sweaters ... and a rather run-down-looking hotel where we decided to go and have a drink. And when we walked into the rather cramped bar, we found half the passengers from the boat in there already! I'm sure the Shetlands have their charm on a fine day but, needless to say, I don't think I'll be making it the first choice for my next holiday!

We then headed straight to Molde in Norway. There, someone else came a cropper. Guest lecturer Brian Lewis gave illustrated talks on the lives of classical composers like Tchaikovsky, and his wife Wilhelmina used to operate the lighting and the slides. They went ashore at Molde and were walking down a steep flight of stone steps when Wilhelmina tripped and fell. An ambulance was called and she was rushed to the local hospital ... but she made it back to the boat — arm in a sling and with a black-and-blue face, poor thing. But she stayed cheerful and insisted on carrying on with her job.

Of course, a lot of accidents can happen on board if you're not careful — slipping on the deck, falling when the boat rolls with the waves ... so it's not unusual to see someone walking about bandaged or plastered at one time or another. We didn't go ashore much, having seen many of our ports of call before, but we did disembark at Bergen in boiling hot sunshine that somehow you don't equate with Norway! When we had previously visited this lovely city we had noticed that one of our favourite 'Thomas the Tank Engine'-style trains appeared to be running so we thought we'd try to find it this time. And what a journey! This little train weaved itself round hairpin bends and roads that were only just wide enough to take us high up into the mountains. Occasionally, we met lorries face to face on tiny mountain roads, but even meeting a cyclist on a narrow pass was enough to cause a traffic jam! But when we finally got up to the top and stopped near a small café for a much-needed cold drink or ice cream, the scenery was quite amazing. But I think what intrigued us most were the people walking about up there, a nun who seemed to have come from nowhere, the odd hiker ... it was miles up the steep country paths and I just couldn't believe they could have walked all the way!

Well, that was our last cruise to date and our talks all seemed to go well, so now we're looking forward to our next destination. While on board the various ships we've certainly heard some funny true stories from the crew which capture the unusual nature of life on board ship. Apparently, the *Ocean Majesty* was cruising around the British Isles and was starting off from some far-flung point in Scotland. One passenger who had decided to join the ship was travelling from his home in the West Country. He had an arduous journey driving up there from one end of Great Britain to the other, and it took him hours but he arrived on time. One of the ports of call was to be the Scilly Isles but, unfortunately, the weather conditions were too severe to dock there so they decided to divert to Falmouth.

While on board, this particular gentleman had been asking about getting newspapers, and when the ship docked at Falmouth and the passengers went ashore, two of the crew members bumped into this man walking along the road. 'Oh, you wanted papers,' they said. 'There's a paper shop just around the corner.'

'I know there's a bloody paper shop around the corner,' he snarled, 'but I'm going home to mow my lawn.'

After his long trek all the way to Scotland, they'd brought him back to where he lived! And sure enough, the man went and mowed his lawn ... and then got back on board.

On another occasion, one of the girls in the crew was walking down a corridor quite late on the last night of the cruise. Everybody, as instructed, had put their luggage outside their cabins ready for collection. As she walked along, she accidentally tripped over one case, and realised it felt incredibly light. Picking it up, and then the other one next to it, she realised there was nothing in them. She knocked on the door of the cabin which was occupied by a rather sweet elderly couple and, to her horror, saw they had clothes strewn all over the cabin.

'But you just said put your cases outside the cabin,' said the wife. 'You didn't say anything about having to pack them!'

As I mentioned, there were a few mishaps and accidents along the way on our various cruises ... but nothing as bad as when I went on a cruise around the Greek Islands back in the Sixties. It was our first night at sea and we were all enjoying a drink in the bar after dinner at around midnight when a call went out, 'Man overboard!' We all rushed out on to the deck — I thought it was a regular part of the cabaret at first — but it transpired that a German girl had been out on deck in the wrong place and had somehow slipped through a gap and fallen in the water. Now, of course, you don't have brakes on ships so you can't just stop in your tracks — we had to circle around. It was incredible — within minutes, about four other ships seemed to appear from nowhere and the searchlights were all over the water. This went on for what seemed like ages and, eventually, it was decided that they would have to give up. We were just about to head away when suddenly someone shouted that they'd spotted something in the dark waters. Yes, it was the German girl who, thankfully, was quite a strong swimmer and had managed to hold her own all this time. The major difficulty then was lowering the lifeboat and getting her into it and back safely; the sea was so choppy, the lifeboat kept banging against the side of the ship. But they managed it incredibly efficiently, and as soon as she was safe and sound and back on board — cold and shaken up a bit but none the worse, really, for her ordeal — she was out and about again within a few hours. The thing that struck me, though, was the horrific feeling you must have if you see the boat giving up and heading away. It doesn't bear thinking about.

It was also on this cruise that I visited the ancient city of Ephesus. We were all marvelling at the incredible history and sights of this wonderful place and remarked on it to our tour guide who was a local girl. She then told us a story that I have never forgotten and am reminded of every time I visit some seemingly wonderful place and feel envious of the people who live there. It rather sums up all the marvellous locations we have been to on our cruises.

She told us there was a man, a very good man, and God came and saw him and said that he'd been so good that he was going to show him Heaven and Hell before he died so that he could choose which one he wanted to go to.

So he showed him Heaven. The skies were blue, the grass was green, the sun was shining, the birds were singing ... it was an absolutely beautiful haven of peace and tranquillity.

And then he showed him Hell. It was exactly the same. The skies were blue, the grass was green, the sun was shining, the birds were singing ... the only difference was that lying around the grass were several nubile young ladies in various states of undress.

So came the day that the man died. And God asked him where he would like to go. The man laughed. 'Well, Hell, of course,' he said. And so God sent him to Hell. And it was just like the Hell we all imagine. The burning flames, the screaming and the wailing — and, as the man was being burned by the overpowering heat, he cried out, 'Why, God, why? You showed me Hell and it wasn't like this! Why?'

And God replied, 'Ah, well, *then* you were a tourist ... *now* you're a native!'

16

Thank God for a Funny Face

Writing my autobiography is not a regular habit. I didn't really want to do it at all because I find it boring talking about myself, but somehow I found myself talked into it by other people. So as it has happened, I wanted to pass on a few things I have learned and conclusions I have reached and perhaps you will see me as I am.

I will tell you what I am not — and hope never will be: a snob, a chauvinist, a Wrexham Football Club supporter or a Tory. The only time I have been close to denying my birthplace was when the city was represented by Gyles Brandreth. I was born in Chester, which is in Great Britain, which is in Europe. And, consequently, I have never thought of applying to be a European, because I am one already! The only Tory I have ever admired was Winston Churchill, who had an unusual quality for a Conservative in that he looked forward instead of backward. He thought we should be involved in Europe, and so do I. And the sad thing is that, were he alive today, he would be drummed out of the present Tory party.

When I was four I was patted on the head by Lloyd-George, a blow from which I have never fully recovered. As a result of that, I have always had an interest in the ladies and the Liberals. I come from a Liberal family and have never found any experience in life that has altered my opinion. A vote for Liberals is a vote for You and Me — votes for Tory or Labour are for Us versus Them. How can they possibly govern when their main aim seems to be to destroy each other? These are familiar arguments for the lively family into which I've married. My father-in-law, Jack Davies, now well into his nineties, is a great debater as well as singing solos, playing the piano, driving the car and walking a few miles every day and is married to the vivacious Margaret, ten years his junior. Equally, my lovely sister-in-law Lynne and her husband Gwilym Jones are interested in topics of the day and family discussions are always animated.

I have always maintained that the social function of the professional artiste is to entertain the public. Amateurs are allowed to do whatever pleases them, but those who expect payment must aim to please. Our wonderful theatres were not built as schools but as places of entertainment.

We need to go back to the days of theatre managers rather than 'artistic directors' whose sole interest is to put on what *they* want rather than what audiences want. This is the reason that, nowadays, theatres require subsidies and, apart from the Arts Council grants, the biggest subsidy is given by the actors who are forced to work for peanuts.

When I was 18, I read a biography of John Barrymore, a member of the famous Barrymore family and a celebrated Broadway star. In his own private life, he was said to be rather a nasty character. One opening night on Broadway, a friend of his was standing in the wings whilst Barrymore was receiving a tremendous ovation.

When he came off stage, his friend remarked, 'I don't understand it. You're such a bastard in real life — why do they like you so much?'

Barrymore replied, 'It's easy. I like them.'

This is something every budding actor should remember.

The only way to learn to act is to do it with an audience. Listen to them, feel them and react accordingly — and play to the people in the back row so that everyone can hear you.

I've always understood critics (after all, I was one myself when I was 16!), and performers should appreciate that critics only write to be read and to gain their own stardom.

Having fallen in love with Shân in 1978, we have been in love ever since. We don't try and change each other, we laugh a lot and accept each other — warts and all. Our love story is worth telling.

Oh, and finally — I *do* thank God for a funny face, and for allowing me to do the work I enjoy so much.